waves

of

creativity

A Gathering of Ideas
on Creating with God

ALLEN ARNOLD

Printed in the United States of America
ISBN: 978-0-578-91737-5 (print)
Second Edition

10 9 8 7 6 5 4 3 2

To: _____

From: _____

Date: _____

Every good gift bestowed,
every perfect gift received
comes to us from above,
courtesy of the Father of lights.

James 1:17 VOICE

For the hearts of Creatives.

When you feel unseen, don't believe it.

When the journey seems impossible, stay with it.

When the pull is to do it yourself,
choose instead to pursue it with God.

When no one seems to notice your work,
know that your creativity matters far more than it appears.

When God gives you a dream, he will see it through.

May this book give you hope along the way.

CONTENTS

Always a Becoming (An Introduction) 1

Waves (A Story) 3

Topics

A

Abundance 19
Art 21
Atmosphere 27
Attitude. 29
Awakening 30
Awareness 32

B

Balanced Life 35
Beginnings 37
Being 39
Birth. 41
Bohemians 45

C

Chaos 46
Co-Creation 53
Comfort. 60
Comparison 62
Competition 64
Control 67
Creation 71
Creativity 75
Creator 83

D

Dance 91
Deadlines 93
Desert 94
Desire 95
Destiny 97
Discoverability 99
Dreams 103

E

Expectancy 111
Experience 115

F

Faith 116
Fame 118
Fast 119
Father 121
Fear 124
Fearless 125
Formula 126
Freedom 130

G

Genesis 133
God 135
Growth 139
Guarantees 141

H

Heart 142
Home 148
Hope 151
Hunger 153

I

Identity 159
Imagination 163
Impact 166
Impossible 167
Inefficiency 170
Initiation 172
Intention 175
Interpretation 176
Intimacy 177
Invitation 179

J

Journey 180

K

Kintsugi 187

L

Language 189
Lessons 191
Light 192
Listening 199
Loss 203
Love 205

M

Messy 209
Motive 210
Mystery 213

N

New 215
Not Yet 221
Now 226

O

Offering 228
Open & Closed Doors 231
Opposition 234
Options 240
Order 242
Originality 244
Orphan 248
Others 250
Overwhelmed 252

P

Pace 253
Passion 256
Path 259
Patience 260
Peace 261
Playing It Safe 263
Presence 266
Productivity 269

Q

Qualified 271
Questions 272

R

Reality 278
Rejection 279
Restoration 280
Rhythm 285
Road Trip 287

S

Seasons 289

Story 290

Stuck 298

Success 305

T

Time 311

Transformation 315

Trueness 319

U

Unknown 321

Upgrade 325

V

Validation 326

Vine 333

Vision 335

W

Wisdom 338

With 340

Wonder 346

Writers 349

Y

Yes 352

You 353

always a becoming

An Introduction

Waves of Creativity is a gathering of ideas about ways to co-create with the Creator of galaxies, oceans, and humming-birds; how to get unstuck in your dreams; why formula never leads to freedom; and what true success means. I hope these thoughts will wash over you, refresh you, and awaken you to a new way of seeing yourself . . . and your art.

Madeleine L'Engle was a brilliant thinker who helped me see creativity with fresh eyes. While best known for her novel *A Wrinkle in Time*, her books on art and faith are perhaps even more fantastical. In *Walking on Water*, she notes that we are "always a becoming." This book is designed to help you intentionally pursue that journey of becoming with God.

A story is always a good place to begin. So I start this book with one that will help you see the power of your creativity. From there, I offer a wide variety of brief thoughts, big questions, and Scriptures on 111 topics that reflect various aspects of this journey of co-creating with God, including Imagination, Competition, Freedom, Wonder, Open and Closed Doors, and Restoration.

If all these ideas showed up at the same party, they likely wouldn't get along. Some encourage. Others challenge. Many are poetic or playful. And there are those that just say it like it is. I hope you'll spend time with each of them, especially the ones that stir you to be more, risk more, and create more.

Savor this journey one step and one thought at a time. Use the white space to add your questions, dreams, and insights. The goal isn't to finish fast, but to spend time with the Creator and become more fully you along the way.

waves

A Story

"Can you see your gift?"

The seven stood side by side on the beach, feet in the water. Faces to the ocean.

Their guide was behind them, watching them more than the water. She waited patiently, expectant.

The students gazed out at the sea, becoming more aware of their surroundings. The setting sun. The smell of salt. The chatter of seagulls. They'd spent enough time with Sofi to know her questions rarely led to an obvious answer.

She walked back and forth behind her students. "So much silence," she said playfully.

"Is the gift hidden?" one asked.

"To some," Sofi replied.

"Is it in the water?" another guessed.

Sofi smiled. "Ah, that is a good question. Is it?"

They squinted at the sea, willing their eyes to see more than was there.

"What do the waves reveal?" she hinted.

The students scanned the horizon, but the ocean was a

perfectly still sheet of blue-green glass.

"There are no waves," one responded. Several others nodded in agreement.

Sofi clapped her hands. "Now we're getting somewhere! Come, we have much to discuss."

The perplexed students turned from the ocean to their guide, amazed to find her already twenty feet away at a fire pit. "Gather around," she said. "Let's enjoy a warm drink together before we continue our journey."

It was becoming noticeably cooler since the sun went down. They circled the fire, palms held out to the flickering flames. The warmth felt good.

She pointed to mugs on a nearby piece of driftwood. "There's one for each of you." The wind played with Sofi's silver hair. She wasn't young but seemed ageless. She filled each cup with steaming black brew. As she did, joy over her apprentices filled her heart. They'd spent much time together over the past months. There was such talent in this group. A painter, chef, surfer, teacher, writer, coach, and architect. A beautiful mix of ages, races, and experiences. An eclectic group brought together by a hunger for creativity and God.

They sat on pieces of driftwood next to the fire pit, sipping the hot liquid.

"This'll get you going," the coach chuckled. "It isn't instant coffee."

Sofi laughed. "Instant doesn't make for good coffee . . . or good creativity. Both need time to simmer." She looked around the group and sensed their sadness. "You're here to receive a gift. Why the long faces?"

"Because we failed to find it," the chef said. "You had us stare at the ocean. Is that the gift?"

She smiled. "The ocean is indeed a gift. But it isn't the one I have for you today."

The teacher spoke up. "You asked us about the waves. That's a clue." He took a drink and let the next words form slowly. "But how can we see what isn't there? Why ask for the impossible?"

Sofi raised an eyebrow. "Why, indeed?"

"Maybe . . . " the surfer started, then shook her head. "Never mind."

The wind swirled around the group, causing the flames to dance. "Please." Sofi looked across the fire at her. "I'd like to hear your thoughts."

"I spend a lot of time out there." The surfer motioned to the ocean. "The waves are never predictable. Maybe you're training us to be wave watchers. Is that our gift?"

"You're getting closer. But we are much more than wave watchers." Sofi scanned their faces to see if hope was rising or falling. "Watching is good. It reveals what is . . . or what may be missing. But watching and seeing aren't the same."

She reached to the sand and doodled a wavy line with one finger. "Anyone can observe what is." Then she moved her palm over the sand-drawn image and brushed it away. "As creatives, we are called to do more. To see what is missing or what could be. And then to call it into existence. That is how our Creator initiated the creation of this world. He entered into the empty void. But rather than watch the nothingness, he saw what could be and then spoke it into being."

The group took in her words. The blowing wind and crackling flame were the only sounds. Some sipped coffee. Others looked down. A few took notes. Sofi waited, comfortable letting the group sit with their thoughts.

"How do we get from where we are to creating more like God?" the writer asked.

"A boat."

The writer's brow furrowed. "A boat is all we need?"

Kindness radiated from Sofi's face. "No, but a boat will get us closer. The next step is something we have to experience out there," she pointed to the ocean. Then Sofi stood and dusted the sand from her hands. "Follow me."

The group set down their cups, put out the fire, and walked along the shore to a small wooden boat about fifty yards away. When they reached it, she handed each student a candle and matchbook. "Put these in your pockets. I'll let you know when it's time to use them."

A few helped her push the boat from the sand into the water. They held the craft steady as the others entered one at a time. The students sat in four rows of two. Once all were in, Sofi took her place in the back.

"There are four oars, two on each side. We will row out to a cave about two miles to our right. The stars will provide some light to navigate."

They saw no other boats on the ocean. The only sounds for the first mile were the oars cutting the water and the creak of the wooden boat.

After a time, Sofi broke the silence. "Oars down. We will pause here." The seven shifted in their seats to better see her. A smattering of stars shone down on the small boat floating on the still water.

"Where are the waves? When we can't see something, we have a choice. We can either say it doesn't exist or we can speak it into existence."

"But," the painter said, "even if there were waves, it's too dark to spot them."

"That would be a problem," Sofi acknowledged, "if we needed sight to see."

The seven looked at each other, unsure what their teacher was getting at.

Sofi's voice rose. "It is time to stop watching and start

seeing. Everyone, close your eyes." She waited until each student had done so. "Tell me, what do you see?"

"Nothing." The coach laughed. "Absolutely nothing." Others nodded.

"And from nothing, I am going to speak something into being. Focus on my voice."

"But we can't see anything," the architect said.

"Then listen to what your eyes can't see."

No one spoke.

"In this age, we haven't just lost our sight. We've lost our voices. Tonight, we will find what has been lost, reclaim what has been stolen. Right here. Right now."

The seven sat in utter darkness as Sofi continued.

"God created from nothing. His voice entered the empty void, yet it didn't return void. The emptiness bowed to his words. He imagined what could be. Then he shaped nothing into something, one word at a time. I invite the Creator to join me here . . . as I follow his example."

Sofi stood and stretched her arms to the ocean.

"Waves awaken!" She spoke with boldness.

The group waited for waves, but there was only silence.

Rain started to fall. Sofi looked to the sky. "A storm is coming. Chaos opposes creation. Keep your eyes closed. And hold on tight."

A wind rushed through the boat, rocking it.

"Waves awaken!" Sofi declared in a louder voice.

Thunder rumbled. Even with eyes closed, the seven saw the bright flash of lightning.

She shouted above the wind and rain to her soaking-wet students. "Creation can be messy. That is part of it. In the middle of the not yet, you must have faith to believe what can be. No matter the chaos that comes against it." She stood defiantly in the storm and raised her arms for the third time.

"Waves awaken!"

The wind ceased. The rain abruptly stopped. And the boat became still.

Then they heard a new sound. One of rising waves.

"Keep your eyes closed," Sofi said.

Gradually, the sound of waves grew louder. The boat began to rock, and several students grabbed the sides.

"Ah, you feel it now, yes?" Sofi asked.

She scanned the faces of her students. "Now that you've seen the waves, you may open your eyes." They did and were in awe of the transformation that had taken place. The ocean was alive with movement.

The painter spoke up. "Sofi, you . . . created these waves?"

"I did. And greater waves will each of you create. But to do so, you must first learn the power of your voice. Chaos tries to sabotage your creativity by stealing each of your unique voices. But the answer isn't to go silent or to say less. We must speak more boldly. When we do, we will make waves."

"Meaning what we say will be controversial?" the teacher asked.

"Meaning what you speak into existence will fill the empty, barren places in this world with beauty, life, and order. But chaos never submits without a battle. You saw that just now." She sat, visibly exhausted from her act of creation.

"Let us continue. We are almost to our destination. With the waves, rowing will be a bit more strenuous for the rest of our trip."

And it was. The last leg of their journey took far more effort. Mist from the waves sprayed their faces. But in time, they saw a rocky inlet to their right. It formed a large cave in the water. The closer they got, the more it seemed they were heading into the wide-open mouth of a giant. One that could easily swallow their boat . . . and them.

"We are here. Maneuver the boat to the right side of the cave mouth," Sofi told the exhausted rowers. "We can exit on the rocky surface here, then enter the cave." The students did their best to ease in, but the waves slammed the side of the small craft hard against the jagged rocks. A few were knocked from their benches.

"I've seen better parking from my ten-year-old," the coach quipped.

Sofi tossed a rope to the coach. "Since your ten-year-old isn't with us, why don't you hop out and tie our craft to that wooden post." He grabbed the thick rope and got busy.

"That post is handy," the surfer said. "Looks like we aren't the first ones here."

She pointed to the cave mouth. "Many find their gifts here."

"In the dark?" the painter asked.

"There is no light inside. Not yet. Follow my lead and stay close to each other. Hold hands and take it slow. We'll gather in the large area about ten feet within the cave."

Together, they entered and then spread out at arm's length. Only then did they let go of each other's hands. The dark felt like a heavy blanket over them.

Sofi entered last. "In here, we have no sight. Yet we have our voices. Let us remember the power of our words . . . and how God's light always overcomes the dark." She paused, the only sound the continual ocean waves. "Well done on making it here. It wasn't an easy journey. Tonight, eleven of us come together for a time of gifting."

"Eleven?" It was the voice of the chef.

"Yes, the seven of you. And me. Along with the Father, Son, and Spirit. Never forget that their presence is always with us in all we do and create. Most associate the Father with creativity, because in the beginning, he created the heavens and earth. But he didn't do so in isolation. The Trinity created together in fellowship. Take it from me, it was a sight to behold."

"I always saw God as the Creator," the writer spoke up.

"How about Jesus? Do you view him as creative?" Sofi asked.

"Sure. Look at his parables," the writer said. "Jesus was an amazing storyteller."

"Yes," Sofi said, "But that wasn't his best creativity. Many miss how all things were created in and through Jesus. He too is the Creator, and"—she winked—"also a really good storyteller. The Spirit also played a key role, entering the chaos and participating in the beginning of our world's creation. Tonight, we acknowledge Father, Son, and Spirit as the creators of everything. We are here because of them."

Her words echoed off the cave walls. She paused a moment to let them sink in, then continued.

The coach let out a yelp and jumped, arms flailing. "Oh man. A big spider was crawling up my arm." His voice was several octaves higher than before.

"You okay there, coach?" the painter asked.

He cleared his throat. "I'm good. Just wanting everyone to be careful." His voice dropped. "We're, uh, not in the middle of a hotel ballroom here. That's all I'm saying."

Sofi glanced at the coach but tried not to grin. "Creativity is not meant to be comfortable. It has always been both risky and costly. To understand why, we must look back before time began.

"God created creativity. Imagination was his idea. But he is a generous Creator, and he shared it freely. When he created the angelic beings, he infused into them the gift of imagination. One of the most powerful angelic beings was Lucifer, who used his imagination to picture himself as God. He then asked other angelic beings to imagine the same thing. And what they imagined soon led to a battle in heaven, with one third of the angels fighting against God and the other angels."

"I could've told them that wouldn't go well." The voice of the architect echoed in the cave. "It's never wise for created beings to try to take out their Creator."

"Yes, Sofi agreed. "They were roundly defeated and thrown out of heaven. Yet even after their tragic misuse of imagination, God remained relentless in his desire to bestow creativity upon his creatures. He knitted imagination into Adam and Eve. And Lucifer, this time in the shape of a serpent, encouraged them to imagine a future independent of their Creator. But once again, created beings used their imagination from God to choose life apart from God.

"Today, we each face the same choice. Will we pursue our creativity with God? Or will we use it to imagine God out of the picture?"

"Why would anyone choose to create without the Creator?" the chef asked.

"Yet most do. Look around our circle." Sofi's voice cracked with emotion. "Our group began with twenty. We are down to seven. It is the rare ones who enter into their creativity actively with God, who refuse to worship their creations more than the Creator."

"I don't ever want to lose what I'm feeling right now," the teacher said.

"Which is what?" Sofi asked.

"A mix of awe and responsibility."

For a moment, no one spoke. The cave was almost completely dark, yet the conversation had changed the atmosphere. A tangible sense of hope seemed to push some of the dark away.

"It is time for our ceremony of light." Sofi took a deep breath. "Though we can't see each other well, we will speak words of life into the dark. I'd like to hear one thing you've discovered about God and creativity in our time together. As you share, take out the candle I gave you earlier and light it."

"May I go first?" the chef asked.

"Yes, please."

He struck the match and lit his candle. "For me, everything changed when I started creating with God rather than just for him. I want to dance with the Creator as I cook in my kitchen. I commit here and now to never create alone again." He lifted his candle high and the others applauded.

The architect went next. His candle blazed with light. "I will not be sidelined by chaos, waiting for things to calm down before I create. I will enter into disorder and bring order from it . . . by creating with God." Cheers echoed off the rocky walls.

Another light. The writer spoke boldly. "I've discovered the power of creating in trueness. In creation, God didn't make Christian oceans, Christian mountains, or Christian elephants, but created everything in its truest form. I will do the same with my stories." More applause.

Next came the surfer's candle. "God is not a God of formula. I won't spend my life playing it safe. I want to create new waves with God. Then surf them together." The room grew in light and in excitement.

The painter held his paintbrush. In his other hand was the brightly burning candle. "In all I do, I vow to never worship the canvas more than the Creator. I want my art to draw everyone who sees it closer to God . . . not to me."

"Yes!" several shouted. The energy was electric.

"My God is a God of freedom." The teacher spoke loudly. "I will infuse my students with the freedom to think. To be curious rather than conform. I will nurture their imagination, not numb it with indoctrination." The cheers were now a continuous roar of joy.

The coach struck his match and brought his candle to life. His tears glistened in the candlelight. "I used to think sports— heck, all of life—was about winning. The final outcome was all that mattered. But now I know winning and success aren't the same. Sure, I want to win. But success comes down to doing what we love with God. That's it." He thumped his chest with his large palm. "Sofi, you've given me my heart back."

The space was now illuminated with light. "Look around you," Sofi said. "One by one, your words and your candles have lit this dark cave."

Each person took in the faces of the kindred spirits in the circle.

"Lift your candles . . . and your eyes." The flames of their candles suddenly increased in power. Each light took on a different color. Purple. Yellow. Blue. Orange. Pink. Green. Red. In that moment, their candles transformed into powerful beacons of light. The vibrant colors illuminated not just the ceiling but the faces and walls around them.

Sofi basked in the light. "Now," she said, "look down."

With the space fully lit, the seven lowered their eyes to the floor. Except there was no floor. They were standing on water.

"I . . . I don't understand," the painter gasped.

"And yet without understanding the impossible, you are doing the impossible. You are walking on water."

"Um, how deep is it here?" the coach asked. "I mean, you know, just curious."

"Why worry how deep the water is when you can stand on it? Walking on water depends more on your faith than your feet."

The painter hesitantly lifted one foot, then lowered it. The surfer danced in place. The architect jumped up and down. Water splashed but he didn't sink.

"Now you are ready to see your gifts." All eyes turned to her. "Don't look at me," she smiled. "Look into the water."

They saw their reflections holding beacons of light. "The gift I offer is the wisdom and clarity to see yourself as God does. As sons and daughters invited to create with him. That kind of creativity will change you. And from there, you will change the world."

"I can't believe how much I've underestimated the power of my creativity," the writer spoke softly. "But after this . . . anything is possible."

"With God, all things are possible. You have the power to create waves. Waves of beauty. Waves of life. Waves of hope. To speak waves where there are none. In the desert. In forgotten places. In chaos. Waves that will wash over this weary world and provide living water to those who thirst."

Sofi went to a wall and took an extinguished torch from a holder. She held it out to the seven. "Each of you, come and light my torch with your candles." They did, and the flame became a fusion of all their flames, a new color that had never been seen and has no name. Sofi used her torch to lead them across the water and out of the cave.

The seven gazed at the ocean. Sofi stood next to them.

"We end as we began, looking out at the ocean. Except now you can walk on water."

"That's quite a change," the surfer beamed.

"Yes," Sofi responded. "None of you are the same as you were last month, or even as you were as you stared into the ocean hours ago. You are always becoming more or less of who God created you to be. And your gifting will follow. You—and your art—are always a becoming."

They savored her words. None wanted this moment to end.

"The boat's gone." All eyes turned to the coach. "But I tied that rope tight. No way it could have given way."

Sofi grinned. "You no longer need a boat."

"Will we see you again?" the chef asked.

"In person, no. But in presence, yes. My name means 'wisdom.' That is who the Father made me to be. He created me before there was a world. I was with the Father, Son, and Spirit from the beginning, cheering and dancing and celebrating the creative process. I am Lady Wisdom. And you will find me whenever you seek wisdom."

"You are . . . "

"I am. Now, you must go. The world has become very dark. It needs the light of your creativity."

They nodded, knowing this was their time.

The seven stepped out, walking on top of the ocean. They headed out in separate directions, toward the unique purposes God had stirred in their hearts. A wave went before each of them, guiding them forward. Each wave reflected the personality and gifting of the person.

Sofi looked at the sky. The darkness was pierced by columns of colored flames that illuminated the night sky. The columns of light were headed to different parts of the world, creating waves of beauty and light never before seen. She looked at her students as they walked, ran, and danced toward their destiny. Because of who they were becoming, the world would become something more as well.

In the days ahead, it would be time to gather another group. But for now, it was simply time to savor this moment. So the four of them did.

Lady Wisdom basked in the presence of the Father, Son, and Spirit as she held her torch high and laughed with great delight.

Lady Wisdom

The LORD formed me from the beginning,
before he created anything else.
I was appointed in ages past,
at the very first, before the earth began.
I was born before the oceans were created,
before the springs bubbled forth their waters.
Before the mountains were formed,
before the hills, I was born—
before he had made the earth and fields
and the first handfuls of soil.
I was there when he established the heavens,
when he drew the horizon on the oceans.
I was there when he set the clouds above,
when he established springs deep in the earth.
I was there when he set the limits of the seas,
so they would not spread beyond their boundaries.
And when he marked off the earth's foundations,
I was the architect at his side.
I was his constant delight,
rejoicing always in his presence.
And how happy I was with the world he created;
how I rejoiced with the human family!

Proverbs 8:22–31 NLT

Abundance

What limits do you place on your creativity?

How much higher might it fly
if you replaced your doubts
with God's unlimited resources?

It begins by pursuing what makes
you come alive . . . with God.

Trying to do it all
in your own strength
leads to striving and scarcity.

Co-creating with God
leads to awe and abundance.

Your art pours from one of those streams,
reflecting your choice.

God never worries about running
out of time or resources.

As his sons and daughters,
why do we choose scarcity
when he offers abundance?

When you experience the loss of a dream,
the lack of being needed,
or an unexpected, significant expense,
it can sure feel like scarcity.

In that moment,
choose to believe in God's abundance.

Even if you can't see it.
Even though you don't feel it.

Art

Creating art is both personal and sacrificial.

It begins with the pursuit
of what brings us life.

But for it to be more than a vanity project,
it must also address a felt need
or point of pain of the end user,
not simply point back to us.

Our art is from us—yet not only for us.

Sanitized art is safe art.

The more honest art is always painted
with the scars of our stories.

The canvas is the place your art
and your heart intersect.

Practice the art of creating and releasing.

Your art isn't mostly about you.

Yes, you play an essential role in its creation.
But if you tie your validation to its
performance or start to think you're the focus,
you put a burden on the art
that it was never meant to carry.

Create—then release and
step out of the way.

You are always becoming
more or less of something.

Your art follows that trajectory.

Over time, your creations are a tapestry,
reflecting various aspects of your becoming.

Our art wants to grow deeper, wilder, truer.

It's just waiting for us to go first.

Artists are forerunners
in their specific area of creative gifting,
bringing something new into existence
that changes the atmosphere
for all who encounter it.

Where are you forging a path
and lighting the way?

Our art is the water that we dive into.

God is the ocean inviting us even deeper.

Ride his waves and you'll never
go back to the baby pool.

The best art simultaneously
disrupts and invites.

It helps people see something in a new way
so they can then experience
life in a new way.

As artists, the gap between where we are
and where we want to be
is always worked out on the canvas.

Predictable art happens
when we follow someone else's
(or even our own)
formula for creativity.

Rather than offering more of the same
(even if that's what your audience expects),
find new paths.

Blaze a trail where there is no map.

Stretch. Grow. Risk.
Then invite us there.

Atmosphere

We complain about the atmosphere around us
when God is far more interested
in changing the atmosphere within us.

You can only change the atmosphere
of the places you have authority over.

Like your home. Your young children.
Your business.

This is not limiting. It is focused.

It is your area of purpose,
the arena where you have been entrusted
to bring beauty, life, and order.

The creative process begins with
creating an atmosphere
where ideas can flow clearly and freely.

Sure, that includes
the physical space around us,
but even more,
it involves the internal state within us.

Attitude

Constantly complaining creatives
are creating the wrong thing.

When the going gets tough,
where does your attitude go?

It's easy to be calm
when everything goes your way.

It's what happens when chaos hits
that reveals your true character.

Awakening

One day, God will make all things new.

That's great for creation.

But may he begin with us.
We need it most.

Stay on the journey of discovery
rather than growing comfortable
and settling into the same.

Surprise us with what's now awakening your heart
rather than give us another serving of what once did.

Show us the view from
the new peak you just climbed rather
than the old, safe one.

Your art has an arc.

It may not be apparent at first,
but over time what you create
will mirror your questions, hopes, fears, and passions.

We can lose sight of what matters most.

We slowly let go of the most
important parts of our story.

We stop pursuing what brings joy.

Then we wake one day and
no longer recognize ourselves.

We remain there
until someone reminds us
to remember who we are.
To awaken to all that awaits.

This is your reminder.

Awareness

Our gifting is fueled more
by who we are than what we do.

Internal awareness needs to precede external acclaim.

Shortcuts aren't helpful.

Have you noticed your best creative projects
reflect themes you're wrestling with
or passionate about?

Creating this way shoves formula aside,
infusing your art with greater authenticity
by reflecting the journey you're walking through,
rather than what's popular at the moment.

Don't create to be known.

Create to know.

Five ways to make today better:

1) Fear less; love more.

2) Remember, you're not in control
and it's not about you.

3) Lose expectations.
Stay expectant for what God's up to.

4) Be fully present to those around you.

5) Don't downgrade your hopes.
Dream bigger dreams—with God.

An unexamined life
leads to shallow creativity.

The more you know your heart,
the deeper your art can take others.

Balanced Life

What is the allure of a balanced life?

Everything isn't equal.

Live unbalanced by spending
an abundance of your time
on what matters most.

The art of soul care
involves regularly saying no to many things
so you can say yes to the people
and projects that matter most.

Getting it all done isn't a realistic option.

Being fully present when it counts is.

The busier life gets,
the more tempting it is
to measure who you are
by what you do.

But that's a trap.

Busyness is a poor measure of significance.

God is more interested in
your internal transformation
than your external performance.

Beginnings

What good is a new beginning
if you are determined to stay the same?

Starting well is admirable
...and not enough.

Finishing well matters far more
but is a lost art in our culture's
pursuit of instant gratification.

God, make a fresh start in me,
shape a Genesis week from the chaos of my life.
—Psalm 51:10 MSG

Too many shiny first chapters unravel
before the last page is written.

I'm talking less about the stories we write
and more about the stories we live.

The first pages of our lives are just the beginning.

The better story is where we're headed now.

We say, "Show me the way. Then I'll come."

God says, "Come. Then I'll show you the way."

Being

An artist is called to be more, not simply do more.

The creative process actually doesn't begin with doing.

There is a deeper foundation.

The first step is simply being.

What you create from that place is always original,
because it is more about who you are becoming
than what you are producing.

I love the wildly counterintuitive ways of God.

The antidote to fear is love.

The way to overcome big nightmares is with bigger dreams.

Esse Quam Videri is Latin for
"to be, rather than to appear."

You'll be amazed at the difference
when you choose to be present,
be real, be vulnerable, and be true
rather than merely appearing to be so.

Birth

You can't rush creativity.

When an idea stirs within, it's amazing.
But the process of bringing it to life takes time.

The art will let you know
when it is ready to be born.

Deadlines and formulas may lead to a faster finish.
But fast isn't the same as a fully realized idea.

To create means to cause something new
to come into being.

What idea are you giving birth to?

What will its presence mean to the world?

Our creativity reveals more about us than we think.

What we give birth to includes both
our strengths and blind spots.

We can't create art that surpasses
our thoughts or imagination.

Where we are faking it,
our art will be less true.

Where we haven't gone,
our creations can't go.

Giving birth to a new idea
is beautiful, messy, and painful.

The goal is creation, not comfort.

Rushing through the creative process
doesn't get you to the right finish line faster.

Getting it done isn't the same as growing an idea.

The act of creation requires the artist to become
good friends with patience, curiosity,
and sleepless nights long before the art arrives.

Being creative involves a certain level
of restless discontent.

That's an appropriate feeling,
because something needs to be born,
and you're the only one who sees it
before it has form.

Until then, it won't let you go
and others won't understand.

Even so, stay true and stay with it.

Setting a pre-determined due date
for when your idea will be done and
when the idea is actually ready to be born
aren't the same.

With the first, you hit a deadline.

With the second, you nurture the idea
until it's fully ready to be born.

It's good to know the difference.

Bohemians

The best creativity is always
done in collaboration—not isolation.

The creation of all we know
happened through the interactive process
of Father, Son, and Spirit.

Our creativity comes alive when we choose
to pursue it with God and with others.

In a world that values formula and control,
the rare bohemians are those
who set aside the way things have been done
for what's never been done.

Chaos

Chaos is a destructive, fear-based force
that prevents you from fully living.

The ways it comes against you
—large and small—
are often intensely personal strikes
meant to leave you empty.

Earth was a soup of nothingness,
a bottomless emptiness, an inky blackness.
God's Spirit brooded like a bird
above the watery abyss.
—Genesis 1:2 MSG

Overcoming chaos is a creative act.

It is the first thing we see
God do in Genesis.

From the first verse, we
meet him as Creator.

His Spirit immediately goes into the
empty void and begins transforming it.

He speaks light. He creates.

Disorder gives way to order...through creation.

Chaos cannot invade your domain
—your heart and your head—
without your permission.

It wants you to believe you have no choice
but to become chaotic when chaos hits.

That's a lie.

Chaos tries to make us forget who we are...
and become more like it.

The Creator reminds us who we are...
so we can become more like him.

I see that the LORD is always with me.
I will not be shaken,
for he is right beside me.
—Acts 2:25 NLT

Those who think they can use chaos
to their advantage will soon
find themselves used.

The chaos they seek to master
will master them.

It's like riding on the back of a tiger
thinking it is your pet,
when actually, you are its lunch.

With God, we can enter the chaos
without letting the chaos enter us.

It's freeing to realize
that chaos comes at us,
but it is not us.

Chaos swirls around us, trying to
end our hopes and dreams.

Creativity stirs within us, ready to
birth new hopes and dreams.

Chaos is primal, but it isn't eternal;
it didn't always exist.

Chaos didn't get the first word
nor does it get the last.

Only God does.

When chaos and the Creator
come face to face,
chaos blinks every time.

Your point of pain
—the current chaos you're going through—
is likely the canvas for your next creation.

The best journey your art
can invite others into
is the costly one you must walk first.

If you're at a loss of what to offer
this chaotic world, here's a suggestion:

Make something beautiful.

Co-Creation

God's desire is to spend time co-creating with you
rather than nodding in approval
at a finished work you did by yourself.

We, the God-created, have unique roles to play
in the ongoing creation of beauty, light, and order.

The invitation isn't to do so
in our limited strength or brilliance,
but in collaboration with
the unlimited resources
and abundance of God.

True creativity isn't dependent on
a degree or reserved for the elite.

No person or organization gets to define
our gifting or act as the gatekeeper of creativity.

God alone has that right.

As Creator, he infuses us with creativity,
then invites us to pursue it with him!

What you co-create with the Creator
has the spark of eternity.

What you create in your own strength
is limited by your limitations.

When you co-create with the Creator,
criticism loses its ability
to validate or invalidate your art.

Experiencing the Creator's presence
in the creative process isn't a nice add-on.

It's the goal

Creating with God is a wild, holy adventure.

He infuses us with our unique gifting.

Then invites us to pursue those desires with him.

It may or may not produce money or fame.

But it always produces change...starting with us.

What we create alone from our own strength
can't surpass our weaknesses.

Yet what we create with the Creator
can't help but transcend us.

Does your art possess an essence that ushers people from their normal into the eternal?

It will when you actively create with the Creator.

The best stories are the ones we co-create with God.

These are the stories that transcend our limitations.
Shimmer with an eternal spark.
Awaken hearts and open eyes.

But they can never be created in isolation.

They require the active presence of the Creator.

We all long for our art to make an eternal impact.

Yet so few creations shine for more than a moment.

What's missing is an eternal spark—
one that comes from the glow of those
who have spent time with the Creator.

Only what is co-created with God has that brilliance.

Co-creation is never a DIY (do it yourself) project.

When is the last time you asked God
how he sees your creativity?

That's between you and him,
but he's always ready to share.

In a world of endless opinions,
his interpretation matters most.

Comfort

Comfort softens your creative edge.

Don't seek a cozy chair and a cup of mocha when you're creating.

Seek a question that won't let you go,
an ache that you can't quite name.

Then wrestle it out on the canvas.

Your art is an attempt to answer through colors, words, and images.

Your art can't take people on a journey of discovery
while you stay comfortably camped in the status quo.

You must first step into the unknown,
face your fears, and discover God in fresh ways.

It requires the humility to be a wide-eyed
traveler rather than master guide.

Great art is often born in the midst of great chaos.

It isn't by accident.

It is the antidote.

Though your finished art might comfort people,
the creation process isn't meant to comfort you.

It is costly,
requiring a sacrifice of time and emotion
as you enter the unknown
with no guaranteed outcome
other than being stretched
beyond what you thought possible.

Comparison

Our culture is all about
comparison, conformity, and control.

Industries set rules and rewards.

Customers want more of the same.

But the bigger question is this:
Are you running the race you were born to run—
even if there's no cleared path, no cheering crowd,
no upfront interest in your art,
and no clear end point?

If not, you'll eventually burn out,
because you're stuck on a treadmill
rather than a path of life.

Comparing is toxic because it either ends up
deflating your heart (mine isn't as good)
or inflating your ego (mine is best).

In the end, it forces all art to resemble what already is.

Which is the exact opposite of how God creates.

His ideas are original and birthed in freedom!

Competition

Creativity is not a competitive sport.

Period.

Your opinion on someone else's creativity
matters far less than
what you actually bring to life.

Spend more time creating than critiquing.

Comparison kills creativity.

You aren't competing with other artists,
so stop measuring yourself by what they create.

Their work is based on their journey;
your ideas come from your journey.

Pursue your passion with fierce intentionality
by focusing on what's in front of you,
not who is beside you.

Another person's victory is hard to celebrate
when it is interpreted as your loss.

The world looks to critique, compare,
and conform our creativity.

The Creator loves to spark, shape,
and smile at our creativity.

Pursue what you were born to create
with fierce intentionality.

Control

You must release the illusion of control
as you step into mystery and
strange new lands with God.

This guarantees the unexpected.

Once you believe anything can happen,
you're open to whatever God invites you into.

Often these will be situations you
couldn't have imagined with outcomes
only possible through him.

We get so busy trying to control outcomes,
we forget that our creativity thrives
in freedom more than forced steps.

Don't mistake tools for rules.

Tools can help artists bring their work to life.

Rules replace freedom
with someone else's formula,
draining life from artists
and their creations.

There is such freedom when you let go
of all your demands of how
your life should go.

Relinquish the script
you've been holding so tight.

Replace it with expectancy for
the story God has for you.

When we feel the world closing in around us,
it's easy to go into survival mode.

We tighten our grip
in an effort to not lose more.

But what if we allow the unexpected and
unwanted interruptions to remind us that
we were never in control in the first place?

We grow most on journeys
where we have the least control.

What keeps us in a small story?

The belief that we can control our lives.

We want safety and certainty.

God guarantees neither.

He invites us into a larger, wilder story.

But we can't enter in
until we let go of our illusion of control.

Once you realize you don't need
permission to create outside the lines,
your canvas will grow exponentially larger.

Creation

In the beginning was the Word,
and the Word was with God, and the Word was God.
He was with God in the beginning.
Through him all things were made;
without him nothing was made that has been made.
In him was life, and that life was the light of all mankind.
The light shines in the darkness,
and the darkness has not overcome it....
The true light that gives light to everyone
was coming into the world. He was in the world,
and though the world was made through him,
the world did not recognize him.
—John 1:1–5, 9–10 NIV

Creation is invitation.

It tells a story about the artist and the observer.

By his Son, God created the world in the beginning,
and it will all belong to the Son at the end.
This Son perfectly mirrors God,
and is stamped with God's nature.
He holds everything together by what he says—
powerful words!
—Hebrews 1:2 MSG

Therefore, if anyone is in Christ,
the new creation has come:
The old has gone, the new is here!
—2 Corinthians 5:17 NIV

How does God create?

Extravagantly. Wildly. Generously. Freely.

In the Genesis creation account,
God didn't need time to warm up or find his groove.

He wasn't irritable during creation.

He wasn't relying on a formula
or hoping nervously that others
would approve of his creation.

He created joyfully and confidently.

Remarkably, he invites us to do the same.

Nothing created can ever satisfy your soul

Not nature. Not the galaxy.
Not a person—nor anything we create.

That's because creation, at its best, is meant to draw you
closer to the Creator, not be the source of your worship.

Sure, enjoy the ocean, sunsets, forests,
and the presence of others.

But don't expect them to complete you.

Only the Creator of all can be your all

Creativity

God-infused creativity is an act
that brings something new into existence
—through our presence and gifting—
that changes people and the atmosphere for good.

Believing that you aren't creative
has enormous consequences.

It closes a door to the future that you were born to
shape through your unique presence and talents.

You. Are. Creative.

How could it be otherwise?

Your bloodline traces back far beyond your parents.

The DNA of the Creator pulses through you.

The One who created sunsets, oceans, and stars
made you to create as well.

The invitation is to do it together.

Creating new things with God starts with
seeing yourself and your art in new ways.

Creativity is not a rare gift
limited to some elite class of artists.

Everyone is born with creativity because
we are all sons and daughters of the Creator.

Humans aren't the original creators
or the official gatekeepers of creativity.

God is.

True creativity always points back to the Creator.

Ultimately all our talents, passions, dreams,
and creativity begin and end with God.

As sons and daughters of God,
we are artisans who have the imagination
of the Creator flowing in and through us.

The best we can do as creatives is invite others
into the ideas we can't quit thinking about.

How could anyone's creativity
not suffer a catastrophic loss
when it is untethered from the Creator?

The art of living well precedes the art of creating well.

We continue to be created as we create.

God shapes us, which then shapes
the canvas we're working on.

From that process, art is created
that has the potential to reshape the world.

Lies that come against your creativity:

· Time is short and you're behind. Hurry or it won't happen.

· You're alone, only valued for what you do. So do more.

· Breakthrough hinges on finding a formula for success.

· If you take a break, fans will move on.

If your creativity were a meal,
would it best be described as leftovers
or an original dish the world has never tasted?

Our creativity reveals so much about us.

It reflects both our strengths and blind spots.

Where we haven't gone, our creations can't follow.

Being called by God to create
and feeling ready to create
are two totally different things.

You will never feel nor be completely ready.

But you can always take the next step as God reveals it.

CREATOR

In the beginning, God created...
-Genesis 1:1 NIV

Christ himself is the Creator
who made everything in heaven and earth,
the things we can see and the things we can't;
the spirit world with its kings and kingdoms,
its rulers and authorities;
all were made by Christ for his own use and glory.
-Colossians 1:16 TLB

Before creating something,
create space for the Creator
to be part of the process.

Do you see God as an active creator?

Sure, he kicks off the book of Genesis
as Creator....and then
proceeds to create everything.

But that wasn't the end of his creativity.

He didn't retire as Creator.

He is the continual Creator. He still creates.
Ask and he'll show you ways to join him.

If the top creative genius in your field
offered to share all he knows with you,
would you want to spend time together
or keep doing it all on your own?

God is the expert at
the very thing you're drawn to.

Not only that, he infused you
with those interests as
an invitation to pursue them together.

But it's your choice
whether to take him up on the offer.

Everything good exists
because God imagined it
and then spoke it into existence.

Whatever we create is only possible because he spoke
us into existence and sparked that talent in us.

For see, I am creating new heavens
and a new earth—so wonderful that no one
will even think about the old ones anymore.
-Isaiah 65:17 TLB

Nothing about God is static.

Even his name is an ongoing verb.

The name Yahweh conveys simultaneous
aspects of past, present, and future.

It is built on the Hebrew word "to be,"
which connotes eternal, ongoing existence.

The God who made the world and everything in it,
this Master of sky and land,
doesn't live in custom-made shrines
or need the human race to run errands for him,
as if he couldn't take care of himself.

He makes the creatures; the creatures don't make him.
Starting from scratch, he made the entire human race
and made the earth hospitable, with plenty of time and
space for living so we could seek after God, and not
just grope around in the dark but actually find him.

He doesn't play hide-and-seek with us.
He's not remote; he's near.
We live and move in him, can't get away from him!
One of your poets said it well:
"We're the God-created."
—Acts 17:24-29 MSG

If you want to know the heart of a creator,
look at what he or she creates.

The One who created you
and gave you the desire to create
has the only true perspective on your creativity.

In a world full of opinions,
give God the first and last word on your art.

Every other opinion offers a limited, subjective view—
sometimes helpful but always incomplete.

Want to infuse your imagination with the eternal?

Invite the Creator into your creative process.

True creativity begins with the Creator.

Desire to know him.
To spend time together,
on walks, in conversation.

Ask him questions.
Share your dreams and disappointments.
Read Scripture. Soak up worship music.
Spend time in movies and books that
draw you closer to him.

The more you pursue God,
the more you will find him in new
and unexpected and playful ways.

The shared experience won't just change your art.
It will change you.

Rather than give you a formula for success,
God gives you himself.

Choose the Creator over man-made rules
and watch your creativity soar.

You are worthy, O Lord our God,
to receive glory and honor and power.
For you created all things, and they exist
because you created what you pleased.
-Revelation 4:11 NLT

Dance

Your creativity should be
an active, intimate dance with God—
something the two of you do together.

Even if the process involves a large team,
save the first and last dance for God.

Sure, there are creative disciplines and rhythms.

But the desire to formulize them dulls the process.

Going through the motions and expecting
the same results is a lifeless way to birth ideas.

See your creativity less as a duty
and more as a dance.

Then go where the music leads.

What makes you come alive?

God gave you those unique gifts and desires
as an invitation to pursue them with him.

To enter into a beautiful dance
with Father, Son, and Spirit
that awakens your heart and your art.

You were never meant to create alone.

Make the shift to with.

The world offers countless songs.

Most cause us to forget who we are.

Only God can write your theme song.

Discover it as you dance with him.

Deadlines

Hitting a deadline with your art
isn't the same as
offering a lifeline through your art.

Make sure what you create isn't just on time—
but has something original to
say when it arrives.

Desert

Your Creative Desert is the place that tries
to derail or defeat your heart and your art.

It is where you are tested,
the arena where your dreams
either disintegrate or are forged anew.

Desire

Your deepest desires,
the very things that make your heart come alive,
actually serve as a source code that draws you to God.

The more you pursue your heart's desires,
the more you discover the One who gave you those
desires so you would pursue them together with him.

Take delight in the Lord,
and he will give you the desires of your heart.
—Psalm 37:4 NIV

As you pursue the stories and songs you are born to write,
realize God birthed them in you.

He did so intentionally.

As an invitation to create the new together.

Destiny

For we are God's masterpiece.
He has created us anew in Christ Jesus,
so we can do the good things
he planned for us long ago.
—Ephesians 2:10 NLT

Stay focused on what's ahead.

You can't ride to your destiny looking backward.

He created all the people of the world
from one man, Adam, and scattered
the nations across the face of the earth.
He decided beforehand which should rise and fall,
and when. He determined their boundaries.
-Acts 17:26 TLB

Pursue your passion.

But don't assume you know the outcome.

You're in the middle of a story
that's still being written.

Who you're becoming
—and why that matters so much—
will only become clear in future chapters.

Discoverability

How do you invite others into your offerings?

"Buy my art because I made it
and need it to sell" isn't compelling;
it's all about you.

Instead, focus on others.

Invite them to join you as fellow travelers
on a shared journey, through your art.

Undiscovered art remains the same piece
of art once it gains popularity.

Yet rare is the artist who remains the same
before and after being discovered.

Yes, artists need to find creative ways
for others to discover their art.

The problem with too much
self-promotion is the "self" part.

It's winsome when others share what
they love about an artist's work.

It's off-putting when an artist raves
loudest about their own creations.

We want others to discover our art.

But first, discover why God called you to create.

With his invitation comes true
creative breakthrough.

No one can do it all.

If self-promotion drains you and limits your creative output, it's probably not a great use of your time.

Imagine if your favorite artist had created more works of art because they spent less time on things others could do far better.

Find experts in what you need done but don't excel at.

You'll be amazed at how everything rises when everyone focuses on their main thing.

The discovery process is finding out what makes you come alive.

It is knowing what you love to do—which isn't always the same as what you're paid to do or even as what comes naturally.

When announcing the release of your new project,
whose point of view do you take?

For you as creator, the work is "finally" here.
Stop everything! Get it now!

For everyone else, they already
have plenty to think about.
Yours is one of thousands of offerings.

If you want to break through the clutter,
share how their life will be better because of your work.

Put the spotlight on them rather than on you.

Dreams

Spend more time remembering
dreams for your future
than limitations from your past.

If God has given you a dream,
he will see it through.

I will pour out my Spirit on all people.
Your sons and daughters will prophesy,
your young men will see visions,
your old men will dream dreams.
—Acts 2:17 NIV

Our creative interests serve as
supernatural homing devices.

God infuses us with unique gifting
before we're born so that we can one day
pursue those desires together with him.

It's not about doing more
but doing what we love to do
with the One who gave us that love.

It seems counterintuitive,
but the way to overcome
your biggest nightmares is actually
with even bigger dreams.

What creative dreams
stir your imagination and passion
but seem too big or impossible
in your own strength?

That's usually a sign of God
inviting you to pursue more of him,
because the only way to achieve
those impossible dreams is together.

Seek him first—and be amazed!

Now glory be to God,
who by his mighty power
at work within us is able to do
far more than we would ever dare
to ask or even dream of—
infinitely beyond our highest prayers,
desires, thoughts, or hopes.
—Ephesians 3:20 TLB

God invites us to pursue our dreams—
with him and without striving.

That's a really good combination.

Don't let others define you
or derail your dreams.

The world needs your creativity
more than it knows.

It needs art with an eternal spark.

"Get over it" doesn't mean
"forget about it."

It means that with God,
you can get over any mountain
between you and your dream.

We were never meant
to pursue our ideas alone.

When we do, we give our dreams
wings way too small for the
places God longs to take us.

When God gives you a dream,
he will see it through.

The way he brings it into being, however,
will likely be quite different
from how you imagine.

Rather than downgrade dreams
that seem too big or impossible
in your own strength,
try inviting God into them.

With him, the impossible becomes possible.

So pursue these dreams together,
realizing God gave you the desires as
a way to draw you closer to him.

Pursuing happiness over joy is akin
to pursuing puddles over the ocean.

Dream bigger dreams...
the kind that can only be realized with God.

Success in pursuing your dreams
without God is actually failure.

The invitation is to pursue
your creativity with God.

That is success.

Expectancy

There's an ocean of difference between
expectations and expectancy.

Expectations reflect what we want
to happen based on our plan.

Expectancy reflects a sense of wonder
and curiosity for God's plan.

It's impossible to be expectant
and controlling at the same time.

Our hands—and our hearts—are either open
or closed to what God wants to provide.

Rather than let unmet creative expectations
fill you with resentment, resignation, or regret,
reset your heart with expectancy for what is to come.

Today could be that very day of breakthrough—
if you show up ready to create.

Those brave enough to carry a travel journal
convey a heart of expectancy.

They are ready to hear from God
and receive ideas no matter where they are.

And because of that, they do.

Before your art can capture the hearts of others,
it must first be set free from expectations.

Your art doesn't validate you.

Only God has the power to do that.

There is never an expiration date on
the promises and dreams God gives us.

But they rarely play out as we expect.

Rather than carve your expectations in stone,
enter each day with a sense of expectancy
for what God is up to, and dive fully into that.

What limitations and expectations
do you place on your creativity?

Imagine how much higher your creations could fly
without that unnecessary baggage.

Expectancy is the key.

Experience

You can't offer others something you've yet to experience.

Leave your comfort zone.

Go into the unknown.

Explore. Risk. Create.

Then let your art invite others to join you on that journey.

Faith

Now is when your faith matters most,
right in the messy middle of having no idea
how things could possibly work out.

If you could figure it out, faith wouldn't be needed.

Walking on water depends more
on your faith than your feet.

But you must still risk that first step
with no guarantees other than God.

The more expansive our faith is,
the larger the canvas we can create upon.

If the best we can do during challenging times is
hunker down and hope for something better and
easier, we miss living fully in every season of life.

The time to trust and risk is now.

Faith isn't needed at the victory party
after the battle has been fought.

It's needed in the middle of the not yet.

Can you be steadfast in the unknown, before you
can see the horizon or know the test results
or understand how the pieces fit together?

Fame

Rather than seek popularity,
seek to make a difference.

Fame is fleeting.

Impact is eternal.

Fast

Go at your pace.

The goal isn't to get somewhere first
or fast but to arrive more fully you.

Don't look for shortcuts to God.
The market is flooded with surefire,
easygoing formulas for a successful life
that can be practiced in your spare time.
Don't fall for that stuff,
even though crowds of people do.
The way to life—to God!—
is vigorous and requires total attention.
Matthew 7:13-14   MSG

The pull is to quick answers and shortcuts—but God keeps inviting us to choose the harder, longer, unknown path.

It's not about the shortest distance
between two points
but the necessary journey
from who you are
to who you're becoming.

It's amazing how God is always on time,
yet never in a hurry.

Father

I will be a Father to you,
and you will be my sons and daughters,
says the Lord Almighty.
-2 Corinthians 6:18 NIV

God is primarily a good Father who teaches—
not a good teacher who occasionally fathers.

Thank you for making me so wonderfully complex!
It is amazing to think about.
Your workmanship is marvelous—and how well I know it.
You were there while I was
being formed in utter seclusion!
You saw me before I was born
and scheduled each day of my life
before I began to breathe.
Every day was recorded in your book!
—Psalm 139:14–16 TLB

This resurrection life you received from God is not a timid, grave-tending life. It's adventurously expectant, greeting God with a childlike "What's next, Papa?" God's Spirit touches our spirits and confirms who we really are. We know who he is, and we know who we are: Father and children.
–Romans 8:15–16 MSG

Fear

Your gifting invites you to run toward something.

Your fear warns you to run from it.

The direction you run determines your destiny.

Fear was never the intended message for our lives—
nor does it get the last word.

Fearless

Light, space, zest—that's God!
So, with him on my side I'm fearless,
afraid of no one and nothing.
-Psalm 27:1 MSG

Formula

Creation is bringing something new into existence.

Formula is re-creation of what has been.

Through a repetitive series of steps,
it seeks to gain similar results
by duplicating what's worked in the past.

That's great for a muffin mix.
Not for your art.

Art born in freedom always transcends
art based on formula.

When people promise success
if you apply their formula to your art,
don't fall for it.

There are no guarantees.

Lightning rarely strikes in the same place twice.

And true success can never be
bottled, tamed, or contained
based on what's worked before.

Formula only leads to re-creation,
never a new creation.

Formula limits creativity because
it can only tell you how to do what's been done.

It looks backward.
Creativity looks forward.

There is no formula to the fantastical.

We can't dissect our dreams or analyze
our way to the impossible.

We can only step into those bigger
hopes and desires with God.

The act of creating is a journey into the unknown.

Enter not as the expert but as a traveler filled with wonder, humility, and expectancy.

You're not trying to repeat history, but make it!

Freedom

It is for freedom that Christ has set us free.
—Galatians 5:1 NIV

Always choose freedom over control,
peace over chaos, love over fear,
and unity over division.

It's not just the right way to live.

It's how God designed our world
—and our hearts—
to thrive.

Losing what holds you back is never loss.

May you find the freedom
to move forward without
the constraints of the past
or fear of the future.

Your art doesn't make you.
You make your art.

Create in greater freedom by
refusing to give your art the power
to validate or invalidate you.

Wherever the Spirit of the Lord is,
there is freedom.
—2 Corinthians 3:17 NLT

Creativity crumbles under the weight
of comparison, conformity, and control.

But it flourishes with freedom.

When you stop trying
to see things like everyone else,
there is freedom to bring to life
what only you have eyes to see.

Genesis

The first two ways God makes himself known
in Genesis are as Creator and Father.

Which means you are the son or daughter
of the most creative being ever.

That's not just a fact.

It's an invitation to pursue
what you love to do with your dad.

I will bring out into the open
things hidden since the world's first day.
—Matthew 13:35 MSG

God, make a fresh start in me,
shape a Genesis week from the chaos of my life.
—Psalm 51:10 MSG

The Bible begins with a Creator creating.

Is there any doubt that God places
a high value on creativity?

God

God's Message, the God who created the cosmos,
stretched out the skies,
laid out the earth and all that grows from it,
Who breathes life into earth's people,
makes them alive with his own life:
"I am God. I have called you to live right and well.
I have taken responsibility for you, kept you safe.
I have set you among my people to bind them to me,
and provided you as a lighthouse to the nations,
To make a start at bringing people into the open,
into light: opening blind eyes, releasing prisoners
from dungeons, emptying the dark prisons.
I am God. That's my name."
—Isaiah 42:5-7 MSG

The life you have with God while creating
determines the power your art will have.

That is because true art is first relational.

Not between you and a canvas
but between you and God.

He wouldn't have it any other way.

God creates us in his image.

May our creations do the same—
reflect his image rather than ours.

That's what gives art its eternal spark.

He is the God of colors, music, flowers,
sunsets, words, and food.

He invites us to see, hear, touch,
and taste that he is good.

Have you ever asked God what he thinks of your creativity?

He is, after all, the one who gave you your talent.

If you've not experienced the beauty and power of this,
just ask. "God, how do you see my art?"

Then stop talking.
Stop guessing.
Stop assuming.
And listen.

Everything.

Following God costs everything.

Yet we don't lose anything.

Through Jesus' life, death, and resurrection,
we gain everything.

And what can separate us from his love?

Nothing.

That's no small thing. It's...

Everything.

Who else has held the oceans in his hand?
Who has measured off the heavens with his fingers?
—Isaiah 40:12 NLT

Growth

The need for continual growth
is within the DNA of every artist.

The hunger for what's new and next
is as essential to our art
as oxygen to our lungs.

Yet true growth is best determined
by who we are becoming.
Not growth in popularity.

The artist's journey is always first internal.

We can never coast our way to true growth.

Climbers can either stop
halfway up the mountain and
build a permanent home
or continue up,
exploring the new.

Artists must make the same choice.

As we grow, our world expands.
The art follows.

When we become stagnant, our world shrinks.
The art follows.

The growth of our craft
begins with the growth in ourselves.

Guarantees

God rarely gives us upfront guarantees.

He seems to prefer inviting us into adventures
that include equal parts faith and mystery.

Bringing something new into existence is rarely easy.

It requires much upfront without any guarantees.

Be content in what you're creating
regardless of the outcome—
or find something else that brings you joy.

Constantly complaining creatives
are creating the wrong thing.

Heart

Guard your heart above all else,
for it determines the course of your life.
—Proverbs 4:23 NLT

※

You can't make another heart beat
faster if yours has flat-lined.

For life to flow from your art,
begin by caring for your own heart.

It is the wellspring of life.

Everything you do flows—or doesn't—from it.

If nothing is more important
than protecting your heart,
how are you intentionally
caring for it each day?

If you can't name specific ways
you are taking care of your heart,
it is likely in need of attention.

No great art has ever been
created without great heart.

The place your heart and
your art intersect is your canvas.

Create from that space today.

Your heart is what the enemy is most after.

And he will throw as much chaos at you
as possible to cause you to lose heart
or give it to the wrong things.

Create in me a new, clean heart, O God,
filled with clean thoughts and right desires.
—Psalm 51:10 TLB

I will give you one heart and a new spirit;
I will take from you your hearts of stone
and give you tender hearts of love for God,
so that you can obey my laws
and be my people,
and I will be your God.
—Ezekiel 11:19-20 TLB

How would you describe
the state of your art?

Now, how would you describe
the state of your heart?

The two are inextricably connected.

A few ways to care for your heart
in this chaotic world:

Make something beautiful.

Do something kind.

Be fully present.

Value God's wisdom over human wisdom.

Choose love over fear.

Home

Your true home is wherever you are
surrounded by those who love you unconditionally,
the place where you never need
to do more to feel less alone.

It doesn't matter where you are.

Until you find home, you remain lost.

When you find home, you're found.

That's the DNA to every great story...including yours.

When you live with God,
you are home regardless of your location.

It is a place that doesn't require you
to do more to belong.

Welcome home.

Home is more than where you were born.

In a mythic sense, it is your "True North,"
where you are headed.

And your art?
It is an invitation for others
to find their true home.

Before you can experience a creative "homerun,"
you need to know where "home" is for you.

How else can you set your sights on it and run to it?

We spend our days either believing life is up to us
or experiencing the wildness of life with God.

You choose which reality to call home.

Hope

"For I know the plans I have for you," says the Lord.
"They are plans for good and not for disaster,
to give you a future and a hope."
—Jeremiah 29:11 NLT

Don't place your hopes for better times
on the change in seasons.

A new page on the calendar doesn't make a new you.
Only God does.

Give him your heart, your dreams, and your plans.

That is where true change begins.

May the God of hope
fill you with all joy and peace
as you trust in him,
so that you may overflow with hope
by the power of the Holy Spirit.
—Romans 15:13 NIV

Hunger

You'll do best by filling your minds and
meditating on things true, noble, reputable,
authentic, compelling, gracious—
the best, not the worst;
the beautiful, not the ugly;
things to praise, not things to curse.
—Philippians 4:8 MSG

Do we hunger more for guarantees...or God?

God offers us life-giving manna for each day—
but ultimately we choose what to fill ourselves with.

If our hunger for more isn't satisfied,
perhaps we're consuming the wrong substance.

Create with the Creator.

Then serve your art to the hungry.

That is enough.

If others don't like it,
that doesn't invalidate the dish.

God is more than able to satisfy
our every hunger with a feast of abundance.

He invites us to a table where our names
are permanently engraved on the chairs.

There is nothing we can do to lose our place
at the table—or earn a better one.

But we will miss this fellowship
if we don't frequent the table.

Deep hunger is never satisfied by shallow things.

Eternal longings can't be filled by the temporal.

The LORD helps the fallen
and lifts those bent beneath their loads.
The eyes of all look to you in hope;
you give them their food as they need it.
When you open your hand,
you satisfy the hunger and thirst
of every living thing.
-Psalm 145:14-16 NLT

Running on empty isn't a good way
to run toward your goal.

Knowing what fuels
—as well as depletes—
your creativity is essential
for keeping your tank full.

Each day, we awake empty and fill ourselves anew.

The choice is yours—to be filled with God
or become more full of yourself.

What do you hunger for most in your creativity?

There is no guarantee of sales,
popularity, contracts, or fans.

But God does guarantee his presence in all
you do...if you seek it above all else.

As humans, we hunger for more.

That's good.

But along the way,
we replace "being more" with "doing more."
That seems the quickest path to attain more.

It's a bad trade.

Sure, we need to get things done,
but productivity is never
more essential than presence.

Jesus replied that people soon became
thirsty again after drinking this water.
"But the water I give them," he said,
"becomes a perpetual spring within them,
watering them forever with eternal life."
—John 4:13-14 TLB

Identity

What we've done never limits who we can become.

Who would you be if the world
didn't tell you who you are?

Your creative best comes from your truest self.

Good mechanics don't define
a car by its current state.

They test what's broken to restore it.

Likewise, personality tests don't define us
but reveal our current state
and how we try to make life work.

Ask God who he made you to be.

The right identity is God-given, not test-driven.

Identity never hinges on what you do.

It is unconditionally based on who you are.

The world didn't give you that identity—
which means it can't take it from you.

Are you an artist when you pick up a brush
and start painting, sell your first work,
or once your art's in a gallery?

Are you an author only when your book is published?

Be who you are born to be now.

An industry doesn't make artists and authors.

It's the other way around.

Your primary identity is
a son or daughter of God.

The world doesn't have the right
to re-name, redefine, or limit you.

Unlike a name or title the world gives,
your primary identity can never be
lost, stolen, or downgraded.

We hide, fearing we're less than —
or wishing we were more than — we are.

We cloak ourselves in costumes to look like everyone else.

But the goal isn't sameness.

We're all in the process of becoming.

Not more like each other but more of our true selves.

Imagination

If your imagination is stuck in neutral,
maybe it's a symptom of a static, stuck life.

You can't create a better
story than you're living.

Most can't fully understand your relentless
pursuit of what's never been imagined before.

But God fully knows.

More than that, he gave you those
restless, eternal stirrings. Why?

Because he knows you alone
can bring them to life.
If you pursue them with him.

Before anything came to be,
it existed first in the mind of God.

It had never been...until it was.

He thought of it and then
spoke it into being.

Neither humans nor our enemy can bring
something into existence from nothing.

Only God can.

Everything that is anything exists because
God chooses to bring his ideas to life.

Your canvas is the place where
your presence and gifting play out.

We are demolishing arguments and ideas,
every high-and-mighty philosophy that
pits itself against the knowledge of
the one true God.
We are taking prisoners of every thought,
every emotion, and subduing them
into obedience to the Anointed One.
—2 Corinthians 10:5 VOICE

Every artist has a canvas—
regardless of what you create.

Rather than seek a larger platform,
seek a larger canvas that
will stretch you in new ways.

Yesterday's canvas should be too
small for what you imagine today.

Impact

Intimacy *with* God always comes
before impact *for* God.

Impossible

"Impossible" is a word we use when our view of a problem becomes more real than our view of God.

"What do you mean, 'If I can'?" Jesus asked. "Anything is possible if a person believes."
—Mark 9:23 NLT

Aiming for what's possible in your own strength
sets the bar way too low.

Simply achieving what's possible is, well, boring.

Why be limited by your current abilities?

Congratulations for doing what you already knew you could do.

What if you instead pursued what the world calls impossible?

The impossible becomes possible
as you invite the Creator into
every aspect of your creativity.

The only way to experience a miracle is
to put yourself in a position to need one.

To have dreams so big that they are only possible with God.

For with God, nothing will be impossible.
—Luke 1:37 NKJV

Inefficiency

Creativity and Productivity can both be good—
but one doesn't necessarily lead to the other.

Often, the path to a beautiful creative act
may be wildly inefficient,
while a highly productive schedule
may lead to lukewarm creativity.

Take the pressure off.

Yes, the to-do list is overflowing—
but all demands aren't equal.

You can only be truly present to one person
or project at any given moment, so give
your best to what matters most.

Choose intimacy over efficiency today.

Letting God set the rhythm of your day can feel disruptive, inconvenient, and inefficient.

It means looking to God,
not the to-do list,
for next steps.

It requires pursuing God,
not past formulas, for new ideas.

Productivity can be good.

But seek first God's presence and pace.

Initiation

In a world where we customize everything to our preferences, we try to do the same with God.

We want to re-shape him into an image
that works for us—and we forget.

He is the potter. We are the clay.
He doesn't change to fit us.

We are the ones being formed by him.

How is God initiating you right now?

Take that journey before inviting others to join you.

Otherwise, all your art can offer is
armchair theory about what others have learned.

When standing between two choices and unsure
which way to go, a good question to ask is
which path will draw you closer to God.

Hint—it's rarely the easier path.

God's invitation almost always involves initiation.

That requires you to stretch
both your heart and art in new ways.

When you're in over your head, embrace it as initiation.

The deep is inviting you to go deeper.

Don't miss the opportunity by swimming
back to the shallow end of the pool.

Sure, the baby pool has less risk . . . but it's also
overrated, overcrowded, and underwhelming.

New opportunities are alluring.

What's missed is how a time of initiation
often precedes next-level invitations.

If you're being tested, stretched, and refined now,
don't misinterpret it as failure.

You're likely being prepared
for a coming invitation
that only the new you can handle.

Intention

Creation isn't accidental.

A sculptor names a piece of granite
while it's still a slab,
then brings it to life with intention.

We may not know how something will
come together, but we do need to know
where we're headed, what questions
we're pursuing, and who it is for.

The same as taking a trip.

You don't know how the journey will play out.
But you do pack differently for
time at the beach and a ski trip.

This approach isn't formulaic.

It's creating on purpose, in the face
of mystery, with fierce intentionality.

Interpretation

When nothing is coming together with your art,
pause and ask God for his interpretation.

Choose breakthrough over breakdown
by tuning in to his voice
above the noise of the world.

Intimacy

God could do most things for us.

He chooses instead to do them with us.

We try to make life work on our own,
but God takes us to new places that
make us more than we were.

His goal isn't efficiency. It's transformation.

I don't want your sacrifices—I want your love;
I don't want your offerings—I want you to know me.
—Hosea 6:6 TLB

We were never meant to pursue the things
we love as a solo endeavor.

Why would we try to create in isolation when God never did?

When this world was created, it was an active
dance between Father, Son, and Holy Spirit.

May our creative process be the same.

With the Trinity, yes.

As well as with others.

We ask God for a plan—because information is our goal.

God invites us into a dance—because intimacy is his goal.

Invitation

God rarely invites us into what we can
do easily in our own strength.

His invitations always include him.

Entering into what's beyond our ability...with him.

Together is the point.

If God stirs a desire in you to pursue something,
he will give you the means to achieve it.

And you will achieve it...
as long as you relinquish demands for
how long it takes, what it looks like,
who gets the credit, and what it will cost.

Journey

When God invites you down a new path,
don't expect him to reveal
all the details upfront.

Answers play out along the way,
not before you begin the journey.

Allow your creativity the freedom
to invite others on a journey
without forcing it to teach a lesson.

When you no longer try
to control the navigation,
you can actually breathe easier
and enjoy the view.

Let your creativity usher people into
the unscripted, unfinished journey
you are navigating now,
rather than some past or future journey.

The most engaging art is created
by those who journey into the unknown.

To get there, you must brave
uncharted frontier and risk much.

After all, formula doesn't work
where no one's been before.

People are waiting to be invited into new ideas.

You just have to go there first.

Our creativity takes us on
the most unexpected journeys.

Our steps become our stories.

Traces of the places you journey as an
artist reveal themselves in your art.

No one else can access that exact combination
because they haven't walked your exact journey.

As you create, infuse your art
with more of who you are, not less.

Unless you choose to stay forever
in a small story,
you have to undertake adventures
where you're no longer the expert.

Advice and lectures fall short.

They offer information
from someone else's journey.

We learn by living.

It's not about being an expert on
the topic you're passionate about.

It's about inviting those with similar dreams,
hopes, and needs to travel alongside you
through your art and experiences.

The best journey your creativity can usher
others into is the one you're currently on.

Don't wait until every question is answered.

It never will be.

Instead, create as you journey.

Be the explorer who shares along the way.

Before we seek a larger platform
for our cause or a larger canvas for our art,
we first need a larger journey
that refines and transforms us.

What we create is an outer expression
of our inner journey.

When the internal journey of discovery stops,
the creative process withers.

We often take a journey
for a change of scenery.

But the best journeys create a change in us.

We begin seeing life one way,
but by the last mile, we're no longer the same.

We don't just arrive somewhere new.

We arrive a different person than we began,
transformed by the journey.

Kintsugi

Kintsugi is the ancient Japanese art
of making what's broken beautiful again.

That process reflects
what Jesus came to do...for us.

When asked his purpose,
Jesus quoted Isaiah 61, saying he came
to heal our shattered hearts and set us free.

The Spirit of the Lord, the Eternal, is on me.
The Lord has appointed me
for a special purpose.
He has anointed me to bring good news to the
poor. He has sent me to repair broken hearts,
And to declare to those who are
held captive and bound in prison,
"Be free from your imprisonment!"
—Isaiah 61:1 VOICE

Scars aren't always surface wounds.

They go deep within you.

But transformation goes even deeper.

Through God's healing,
the scars of your story can become
the source of your strength.

Is your art fueled more by the broken
or healed places in your life?

Let God's presence replace pain
as the catalyst for your creativity.

Language

Jesus looked at them intently and said,
"Humanly speaking, it is impossible.
But with God everything is possible."
–Matthew 19:26 NLT

You speak a new language
through your creativity with God.

It transcends words by way of the heart.

The enemy speaks darkness, shame,
and accusation over us.

His native language is one of lies.

God speaks light, grace, and freedom
over his sons and daughters.

His native language is truth.

Whatever form your art takes,
make sure it ultimately reflects what's true.

Lessons

Does your art expect others to sit for a lesson from you—
or invite others on a journey of discovery with you?

Light

And God said,
"Let there be light,"
and there was light.
–Genesis 1:3 NIV

The light shines in the darkness,
and the darkness has not overcome it.
–John 1:5 NIV

Our art shines bright when we co-create with God.

Yet it dims when we create alone
from our limited light.

The Lord wraps himself in light as with a garment.
-Psalm 104:2 NIV

You're here to be light, bringing out the God-colors
in the world. God is not a secret to be kept.
We're going public with this, as public as a city on a hill.
If I make you light-bearers, you don't think I'm going
to hide you under a bucket, do you?
I'm putting you on a light stand.
Now that I've put you there
on a hilltop, on a light stand—shine!
-Matthew 5:14-15 MSG

For what do righteousness and wickedness have in common?
Or what fellowship can light have with darkness?
-2 Corinthians 6:14 NIV

When God lights our creativity,
it is not primarily to shine on us
but to warm others with sparks of eternity
that point back to the Creator.

Creativity isn't meant to be
a mouthpiece for what's popular.

It's meant to be light, not a mirror.

May your art be a voice in the wilderness
that breaks through the matrix.

Stay true. Stay you. Shine bright.

Think of your creativity as a sword
created with God's light.

This weapon of light grows brighter and sharper
as you grow in your art with God.

When wielded properly, it pierces the darkness.

It overcomes fear with love.

It causes chaos to crumble.

If our art just points back at us,
we're shining the light in the wrong direction.

You can't fight darkness with darkness.

It's never smart to become more like
the very thing you're seeking to defeat.

For once you were full of darkness,
but now you have light from the Lord.
So live as people of light!
For this light within you produces only
what is good and right and true.

—Ephesians 5:8 NLT

The times in your life that force you to
ask bigger questions and seek deeper truth
fuel your art to shine brighter.

The shame and accusations that weigh us
down grow larger when hidden—but fade
when exposed to God's healing light.

God transforms our wounds
into weapons of light.

Listening

We've lost the art of listening well.

We want to be heard.

We grow restless with silence.

We demand quick answers.

In the process, we miss each other's
hearts and stories.

We forget how to have conversations
that aren't about us.

Then we wonder why we're lonely.

Want a simple way to grow your creativity?

Practice the art of talking less and listening more.

When you talk, you're just sharing
what you already believe.

There's no learning.

But when you listen, you're exposed
to new ideas, thoughts, and needs of others.

You grow by listening. Your art follows.

Dallas Willard recommends
the powerful spiritual practice of
not always having the last word in
a disagreement or argument even when
—perhaps especially when—
you are right.

Those who loudly proclaim in a conversation,
"The bottom line is this . . ."
rarely place their own bottom on that line.

They are so busy talking that
they forget how to listen.

Yet when we quit asking questions, we calcify.

A little humility gets you further
than a lot of hot air.

It's impossible to learn when you're talking.

You're just re-stating what you already think.

For new ideas, talk less and listen more.

When we talk, we state what we already think.

When we listen, we hear new
ideas and see life afresh.

Honor others by being fully present.

Listen to their dreams, disappointments, and questions
without challenge or correction
or immediately sharing your opinion.

If you're convinced you already have
all the answers and are generally
the smartest person in the room,
you leave little opportunity to learn,
grow, or be surprised—
from God or others.

Loss

Each season brings with it some loss,
much of it beyond our control.

But we can also be intentional
about what we want to lose.

Here are some good options:
shame, unbelief, hopelessness,
resignation, and isolation.

May we lose big on these fronts.

Losing heart isn't good.

But the phrase is also revealing:
what's lost can be found.

If we look in the right place.

When you feel you're losing
heart, look to God.

He's really good at healing broken hearts.

Losing isn't bad when what
you're losing is fear.

Enter into your creative process today
without fear of failure or rejection.

Let go of self-doubt.

That's the right kind of loss.

Love

For I am convinced that nothing can ever
separate us from his love. Death can't, and life can't.
The angels won't, and all the powers
of hell itself cannot keep God's love away.
Our fears for today, our worries
about tomorrow, or where we are
—high above the sky, or in the deepest ocean—
nothing will ever be able to separate us
from the love of God demonstrated by
our Lord Jesus Christ when he died for us.
—Romans 8:38–39 TLB

The best way to overcome toxic fear is with bold love.

Every choice we make is based on Love or Fear.

Fear-based reactions include
control, offense, rage, and scarcity.

Love-based reactions include
grace, hope, expectancy, and abundance.

Love or Fear.

Those are your two choices.

Which do you—and your art—reflect?

In your creativity, discover ways
to pursue what you are for
rather than what you're against.

Love is a better catalyst than fear.

In a contest between love and fear,
it's easy to doubt whether love can win.

We worry that in direct combat,
love may get its tail kicked.

Thankfully, Scripture reminds us that
nothing is more powerful than love.

Three things will last forever
—faith, hope, and love—
and the greatest of these is love.
–1 Corinthians 13:13 NLT

You were never meant to pursue
the things you love as a solo endeavor.

Invite God and others into the process
and never create alone again.

When you get down to it,
only two things really matter:
Love God. Love others.

Messy

The power of our art doesn't begin in the studio or on a page but as we wrestle through a struggle, belief, or loss.

We work it out on the canvas.

It's hard, beautiful, and messy.

As creatives, we understand ideas are works in progress.

Shaping the ideas takes time, patience, and skill.

Yet we often miss that we are the Creator's idea—works in progress being shaped into our truest form.

It's how all masterpieces are forged.

Motive

Why do you create?

Rather than expect your art to do things for you,
let it be an invitation for others
to experience ideas with you.

What do you most seek from your art?

Popularity?
Transformation of those who experience it?
Greater intimacy as you create with God?
Income? Success? Play?

All options aren't equal.
It's good to know and name
what most fuels your creativity.

There isn't a guarantee of income
from our area of creative gifting.

A painter may need to build decks to pay the bills.

A deck builder may need to paint for income.

At our deepest level, we don't create because
we're paid to do so but because we're born to do so.

Don't downsize your gifting
but do release it from revenue results—
and watch both increase.

A healthy motive results in
less pressure to prove something
and more passion to create something.

Your motive for creating
defines the criteria
for how you evaluate success.

Choose wisely.

Artists are often asked, "What are you creating?"

A better question is "Why are you creating?"

Passion, curiosity, and joy fuel your creativity.

Striving for validation or chasing big money drain it.

Take time today to revisit your Creative Motive.

Mystery

To experience the fantastical,
we must step into mystery.

~

Common sense is good as far as it goes.

But God often invites us into mystery
and surprises us with uncommon solutions.

Common sense without God
simply leads to a common life.

What kind of life do you want—
a safe, predictable one or a story filled with
mystery that forces you to lean into God?

Which do you think will transform you
into a person of depth and wisdom?

Which life will people remember and talk about
around campfires a hundred years from now?

New

What would you see,
perhaps for the first time,
if you took a fresh look at your
assumptions, expectations, and limitations?

Ask God for that new vision.

When searching for your next idea,
travel new roads with God.

It's the rare trip where you'll return
with less baggage than when you started.

Do what's never been done.

Not what's been overdone.

The last thing we want is
more of the status quo.

What's needed is an infusion
of the fantastical.

A shift into something so beyond our dreams
that it could only be seen as miraculous.

It feels good when the world
applauds a new invention.

We take that as a cue to make more of
the same thing...expecting the same reaction.

What we miss is that the world
was actually applauding the "new"
rather than asking for more of the same.

Uncharted journeys can only be taken once.

Why are so many books, songs, movies,
and shows today so similar?

Because when something works,
the pull is to produce more of the same.

But what made the first one work
was its blazing originality.

The act of repeating never
matches the art of creating.

God invites us into the "new"
by putting us in the middle of
what we never imagined doing,
only for us to discover we now
can't imagine doing anything else.

We tend to remain the same
until someone disrupts the status quo
and shows us a new way
to see the world and ourselves.

How does your art usher us into the new?

Give your ideas space to run free
without being too quick to define,
tame, or reign them in.

Rather than dismiss something the world
has no name for, give it time to develop.

The first of anything
rarely comes out fully formed.

Not Yet

Ask me and I will tell you
remarkable secrets you do not know
about things to come.
—Jeremiah 33:3 NLT

The middle of the not yet
is the place where your dreams
haven't come true,
risks haven't paid off,
and the outcome is uncertain.

That's the very place
your heart and your art can be transformed—
if you'll persist rather than lose hope.

Most art, like a mirror, just reflects the known.

A higher, more eternal goal is
to see your art as a looking glass.

Give your creativity permission to reveal
what could be and riff on the not yet.

Create in the uncharted realm of the not yet.

Even if no one is asking for it.

Even if there's no applause.

Do it anyway, knowing there are those
who will be drawn to it...once it's born.

Our creativity doesn't end
when we pass from here to everlasting life.

In the coming kingdom,
we'll realize our gifts even more deeply.

And we'll get to enter into them
with much greater freedom.

This is merely our test flight.

A time to practice, refine, and stretch.

But know that more is coming...even if not in this life.

When God opens your eyes to the unseen,
enjoy the view...but don't stop there.

Let your art be a window that gives others
a glimpse into the eternal and not yet.

God longs for us to come alongside him
and step into the unknown and not yet
with no expectations other than
his steadfast presence.

Art that reflects reality is fine.

But you have the chance to do more...
to give people a glimpse of what could be.

Most art lulls us to lower our expectations
and embrace what is.

Rare is the art that invites us to raise
our vision to see what could be.

Be that rare artist.

Now

These are not ordinary times.

Thankfully, God created us for such a time as this.

The only question is
whether your creativity
will change the atmosphere for good.

It's a great day to
love more,
risk more,
play more,
and allow others
to know you more.

We are called to create the new and not yet
but our space to do so is limited to this very moment.

Right here, in the now.

So be fully present to this moment in time,
especially since you can't relive
yesterday or live tomorrow today.

From that space, dream how to make
this present reality a better reality.

Offering

Your creativity has the potential
to become an idol if you look to it for validation
or cling to it as your primary identity.

The best way to avoid this trap is
to put your art on the altar.

Give it to God as an offering.

That releases its hold on you.

You no longer own it...and it no longer owns you.

Creating art is a sacrificial act.

What have you had to sacrifice
to bring it to life?

What you create for others needs to provide
a promise or address their point of pain—
not simply point back to you.

For that to happen, you have to
know what others need.

Relationship comes before creation.

There often exists a tension between knowing your
gifting and finding a way to make a living from it.

If the pressure of making your art profitable
drains too much life from the process,
it may be time to find another revenue stream
so your art can simply be a stream of joy.

Are you creating this project
for yourself or for others?

If it's for you,
use your favorite colors.
Customize every detail to your liking.

But if it truly is for others,
your creation needs to address their needs.

It's no longer your thing.
It's an offering.

Open & Closed Doors

Using open and closed doors to determine
next steps is a dangerously flawed approach.

It lets doors determine your future rather than God.

He may be showing you how to unlock a closed door.

Or teaching you the practice of patience.

Shift your eyes from doors to God . . . and ask him.

Not every open door is from God—
while some closed ones are.

And the enemy has endless doors of distraction.

The goal isn't an open door . . . but the right door.

Choices are like dominos.

Tip one over and it sets in motion
an entire series of events.

They often fall in the most unexpected ways.

Doorways are much the same.

They lead to some options and limit others.

Enter with eyes open.

When facing a problem,
we think the only outcomes are the ones we see.

Rather than simply choose between options A and B,
ask God what he's up to.

He has limitless options that are never predictable
and always better than our attempts
to make things work.

When unsure what choice to make, consider which
has the potential to draw you closer to God—
not which is the most familiar or comfortable.

Opposition

Creation and Chaos are in opposition.

One is a hopeful force that breathes life,
the other a destructive force
that leads to loss.

Your art is where those contrasting
(but not equal) forces play out.

Our enemy is a fallen creation.

He opposes those who embrace their identity
and pursue their creativity with God.

He chose the wrong story
and wants us to do the same.

The most exciting part of a story occurs when the hero comes face to face with an impossible challenge.

We lean in because it's where growth, victory, and breakthrough occur.

So why do we try so hard to avoid similar moments in our own lives?

We have an enemy who seeks to steal, kill, and destroy (John 10:10).

Whatever he is trying to take from you, know this:
A skilled thief never sets out to steal something of no value.

When you find yourself struggling
with an issue you thought you'd overcome,
it's helpful to view the journey more like a
spiral staircase than a trip
from point A to B.

Yep, you've already made one circle
around the issue.

That you're facing it again
isn't always failure.

Perhaps God is giving you
a new pass around the issue,
this time at a deeper level.

In a world of constant distraction,
you have to turn down the noise
to tune in to what matters most.

Infuse your creativity with greater authenticity by using your canvas to explore a current theme or idea you're wrestling through.

Doing so invites others into the journey you're walking through rather than just talking about.

Don't give up on the project that isn't coming together.

Being in over your head is God's way of taking you —and your art— to deeper places.

Rather than vilify those
who hold a different view,
how about calmly explaining
why you think your stance is better?

Outshouting the opposition never works.

Instead, practice the lost art of humility.

Talk less. Listen more.

Seek to love more than win.

Trade rage for grace.

Some of the heaviest things we
carry are regret, fear, and worry.

Bid them farewell and toss them to the side.

Losing what's held you back is never loss.

Culture can never cancel God's creativity.

They can only cancel their participation in it.

Options

When a situation looks impossible,
that's a sign we're not seeing it as God does.

Our limited view indicates there are
only three options, none good.

Yet God has endless options.

In those situations, don't trust your eyes.

Ask the God of infinite possibilities for a vision upgrade.

Cheap in the short run is always
more costly in the long run.

An extraordinary life is never achieved
through ordinary choices.

Order

Order is always harder to create than disorder.

It takes no talent to tear down what is.
Destroyers rarely have blueprints for rebuilding
from the rubble of their own disorder.

Pursuing order is a creative act
that restores things back
to God's original intention.

Some people see a puzzle as a jumbled box of chaos.

It's really a box of purposeful creation,
separated into hundreds of pieces.

The invitation is to discover its beauty
by bringing order to it—
one piece at a time.

Originality

When you create the first of something original,
the world rarely knows how to categorize it.

Don't misinterpret the initial confusion or questions
as a sign you did something wrong.

You did something new
and the world needs time to catch up.

Be patient
but stay passionate.

Humans aren't the originators
or gatekeepers of creativity.

God is.

Playing it safe produces common creativity...
and a common life.

The goal is never to create more like someone else.
To be the next _____.

We already have that flavor,
color, story, and sound.

Giving us more of the same is
at best a pale imitation.

Instead, let your art blaze with originality.

Give us that.

Trying to repeat your past success
by offering more of the same isn't creation;
it's re-creation.

Don't believe that your next breakthrough
requires you to recapture the same lightning
in a slightly different color bottle.

What made the first thing work
was its shimmering originality.

That can never be bottled.

When stuck creatively, artists often hesitate,
duplicate, or terminate the project.

Choose instead to originate.

Let go of how it's supposed to be done
so you can fully pursue what's never been done.

Orphan

You can believe in God
and still miss life with him.

You can know about God
and still live as an orphan.

If you feel alone in your creative pursuits,
invite God and others to join you.

Those in Creative Fellowship
never create in isolation.

What we create solely in our own strength
is weighed down with our blind spots and limitations.

What we create with God
is infused with
infinite possibilities
and an eternal spark.

Others

Art created in isolation isn't all it could be.

Creative Fellowship involves you and God—
and you and others.

Leaving either out leaves your art incomplete.

We do ourselves a disservice
when we think the only time we need others
is to buy or praise what we created.

They are meant to be
part of our creative journey.

The enemy tries to isolate us
from God or from each other.

Neither loss is acceptable.

We need relationship with God.

That comes first.

And we need relationship with others.

That has to follow.

Choosing one while losing the other
is less than what we were created for.

Overwhelmed

The project you're about to quit
because it's just too much?

Try pursuing it with God—
inviting him to overcome what feels overwhelming.

We've all faced situations where we feel
simultaneously overwhelmed with life
and yet underwhelmed with what it has to offer.

That's because nothing in life
other than God
can fully satisfy us.

Only God can simultaneously calm an overwhelmed heart
while awakening it with expectancy.

Pace

Some prefer a fast pace.
Others go slow and steady.

Neither speed is magic. Either can trip you up.

Following God means going at his pace.

Pausing when he slows.
Accelerating when he picks up the pace.

The key is keeping your eyes on him more than the to-do list.

Our pace should align with God's design for what brings life.

We tend to be deadline-driven.

If you want your art to have more life,
focus less on the deadline (a "line of death"?)
and more on the lifeline it can be
to all who experience it.

If your pace of life is crazy,
it's good to remember God never set that schedule.

His pace is easy but he gives you
the choice of how to arrange your days.

Yet he makes clear that the care of
your heart is the top priority.
It comes above everything.

Does your schedule reflect that approach to life?

Let the rhythm of your day be driven less by your to-do list than whether you're fully entering into each moment with God.

In a race, you follow a course with all runners headed in the same direction according to pre-set rules.

As their pace increases, it seems yours should as well or you'll be left behind.

But your unique gifting isn't a competition.

You're forging a new path that doesn't exist until you create it.

So go at your pace.

The goal is to finish well...not fast.

Passion

Before art can stir the hearts of others,
it must first make the artist's heart beat faster.

Popularity and influence aren't the same.

The shallow end of the pool is popular but offers
nothing for those eager to experience the ocean.

Stay true to your passion
and create from that sweet spot.

Fewer followers doesn't mean less influence,
as long as you take them deeper.

Don't let the things you don't like
become your main focus.

Doing so is a bit like the person so irritated by dogs
doing their business in his yard that he posted signs
of a squatting dog with a big X over it on his lawn.

The very thing he least wants is now the most
prominent, permanent fixture he sees 24/7.

Let your art invite us more
into what you love than what you oppose.

Knowing what you love to create is important.

Knowing how to pursue
that creativity with God—even more so.

Creativity is not just something you do.

Your art reveals your deepest longings.

It tells a story...about you.

Not just the piece you're working on today—
but collectively an arc is being built
song by song, book by book, painting by painting.

That deeper story is worth knowing.

Creativity, in and of itself, is never the end goal.

Our creative interests are meant
to serve as supernatural homing devices,
drawing us closer to God.

As we pursue the gift, we come to know the Giver.

But that requires us to be more passionate
about God than whatever we're creating.

Path

Stand at the crossroads and look;
ask for the ancient paths,
ask where the good way is,
and walk in it,
and you will find rest for your souls.
—Jeremiah 6:16 NIV

Easy and best
are rarely found
on the same path.

Patience

When we demand instant results,
impatience gets in the way of the eternal.

Peace

I have told you these things,
so that in me you may have peace.
In this world, you will have trouble.
But take heart! I have overcome the world.
–John 16:33 NIV

Jesus says we are to take heart because he
has already overcome the entire world.

It's the difference between a ship's captain saying,
"In this sea are icebergs, but don't worry,"
and "Don't worry, because I've already
overcome this entire sea."

Jesus comes to give us peace.

Not peace dependent on a peaceful world.

But peace in the middle of a shaken world.

For God is not a God of disorder but of peace.
–1 Corinthians 14:33 NIV

Playing It Safe

Playing it real and playing it safe are worlds apart.

The way you've always done something
isn't a reason to keep doing it that way.

That's playing it safe.

Give us something new next time that stretches you,
that is unproven, and that carries risk.

That's the difference in creating versus repeating.

Clinging to the familiar
ultimately leads to formula.

You can't fully enter into a time of change
if you're determined to stay the same.

The current hard times are preparing us
for coming opportunities.

But we'll never be ready for what's next as long as
we continue to camp in the status quo.

We long for our art to take us
to new and uncharted places.

But the blank canvas
looks back at us and says,
"No, you must go there first."

Presence

More popularity feels good, but is fleeting.

More productivity gets things done, but is draining.

Only more of God's presence fully satisfies.

Which do we crave more,
our plans or God's presence?

The answer plays out in how we spend our days,
where we seek validation, and why we create.

Your presence is more powerful than your gifting.

What you do flows from who you are.

The more we seek God's presence,
the more our world expands.

God didn't create you to do things
for him but to experience life with him.

Embrace that and you'll focus far less on
your productivity and far more on his presence.

Loving God and others well is your primary calling—
not the to-do list.

Measure your days by that compass.

Do we spend more time savoring our relationship
with God or making our requests to God?

May we desire God's presence
far more than his performance.

Productivity

How do you decide if your day was a success?

Is it based on how much of the to-do list got done?

When productivity is your filter,
you can miss God's presence.

God didn't create you primarily to do things
for him but to experience life with him.

Make time for that above all else.

Is a highly driven way of doing life wrong?

It depends what's driving you
and whether you've gotten stuck at that pace.

Always pushing for more at maximum speed
isn't the best gear for a car . . . or a human.

It's easy to pick up unhealthy habits to get things done,
but it catches up over time.

The cost is immense.

Especially when we trade time
to restore with family and God.

When that happens, we become less to do more.

Over time, we no longer know who we are.

The creative process isn't
mostly an act of productivity.

Doing something efficiently and creating something
with an eternal spark aren't the same thing.

One is a breathless race against time.
The other requires time to breathe.

Qualified

Don't wait until you feel qualified to create.

An idea only becomes a reality
as you pursue it.

Once you start, you discover
more along the way.

The goal isn't to have all the answers.
It's to be willing to go where
the questions lead.

Creativity beckons you.

The invitation isn't based on your experience.

It doesn't ask for your credentials upfront.

It just asks you to try what brings you joy.

Questions

Savor big questions over quick answers.

Spend time in that space.

Create from that space.

Then invite us there.

Your creativity isn't a test but a process of discovery.

Questions aren't in the way.

They are the fuel.

A drowning person doesn't consider the origin
of water as they're gasping for air.

It's best to ask big questions before turbulence hits.

Rather than answer our every question upfront,
Jesus simply invites us to journey with him.

Go where he leads.

Discover along the way.

Be satisfied by his presence more than our agenda.

The worst thing to pack for a journey into the unknown—
preconceived answers and assumptions.

The best thing—really good questions.

Because nothing is the same as it was
on your last trip, including you.

Pack wisely.

Some songs offer lessons
while others ponder life's big questions.

Which would you rather sing?

When we think we have all the answers,

we miss the chance to learn,

think new thoughts, or be surprised.

When we try to be the smartest person in the room,

our creativity shrinks.

It grows by asking good questions, staying curious,

and retaining a sense of childlike wonder.

If we refuse to go further

until all our upfront questions are answered,

we'll forever remain right where we are.

Stubbornly stuck in the unknown...

and still without answers.

Instead of grasping for quick answers,
let's grapple with deep questions.

Take the pressure off yourself
to create from a place of answers.

Instead, let your art invite us
into your journey of questions and discovery.

Sometimes we get so focused on having the answer
that we miss hearing the question.

You don't need to be the expert on a topic
to invite us into your journey of discovery.

Be you. Be real. Be original.

Those with similar questions will follow your lead.

Reality

The first step in seeing with new eyes is to let go
of the belief that your current reality is the only reality.

Original art is never born by following a formula.

Creativity isn't limited by current reality.

It re-defines it.

Rejection

A rejection of your art could mean
it wasn't meant for that person.

Or it may be a sign your vision requires
more hard work before it's ready for prime time.

The first option requires grace for the other person.

The second—grace for yourself.

If you downgrade the worth of your art
based on the reactions of others,
you're giving them way too much
power over your gifting.

Restoration

Restoration is a necessary part
of the creative process.

If you constantly race from one project to the next
—never building in time for rest—
you'll end up weary and worn out.

We live in busy times.

But we don't have to live hurried lives.

We choose the pace of our souls
and the rhythm of our hearts.

Calm is possible in the chaos,
but only when we refuse to let it change us
and instead choose to change it.

Restoration is the inconvenient,
inefficient pause we need but rarely seek.

We minimize rest to maximize output.

We push ourselves to the limit, pass out,
and hope we wake up replenished.

That's a recipe for implosion
rather than a rhythm of rest.

We know when we're running on empty.

Yet we give far less attention to
what we fill our emptiness with.

When we settle for quick relief, we end up with
mind-numbing distractions or secret addictions.

When we seek restoration in those empty places,
we become more whole.

The choice is ours.

We don't need you exhausted.
We need you creative.

It's impossible to breathe life into your art when you're having trouble catching your own breath.

Creation has restoration built into it.

God created.

He made stars, oceans, light. He made time.

And then he rested, taking time to enjoy and savor all he had brought to life.

Be as intentional with your restoring time as you are with your creating time.

Being overly available at all times
results in being overly exhausted at all times.

God has designed our souls to need
regular times of restoration—
and that only occurs when we allow ourselves
to be unavailable, at least for a moment,
to the world's non-stop expectations.

When we stop seeking relief,
we can begin pursuing restoration.

Rhythm

Following God means going at his rhythm
regardless of how fast or slow that may seem
to the rest of the world.

God doesn't give us more
than we can do in a day.

We give ourselves that burden.

Better to live simply and get by on less
than trade what matters most
for more money or fame.

The process of co-creating with God resembles
the rhythm of an impromptu dance
more than the efficiency of an assembly line.

The artist must lose the illusion
of control to go at God's pace.

The goal isn't to finish fast
but to be fully present
to what God is inviting you into.

Road Trip

God often invites us down new paths
with no upfront promises or guarantees.

If we refuse to go without all the details,
we miss the road trip.

Every hero's journey, including ours,
reaches that moment where we either cling
to the known or move into mystery.

What new places could our art take us to
if we traded the well-traveled paths we've been on
for a road trip with God into the wild unknown?

How would things change if you saw your entire life
as a road trip with God, a Father inviting
his son or daughter on an epic journey?

God always knows where he's going.

He determines the pace,
the rest stops,
and the scenic detours.

He knows the best route.

Not just to get you where you're going.

But for you to be the truer you when you arrive.

Seasons

God regularly invites you into
new seasons with your life and art.

What's often missed is that this invitation
requires new times of initiation.

Are you aware of how God is initiating you
in this particular season?

Story

The disciples came up and asked,
"Why do you tell stories?"
[Jesus] replied, "You've been given insight into God's
kingdom. You know how it works. Not everybody has
this gift, this insight; it hasn't been given to them.
Whenever someone has a ready heart for this,
the insights and understandings flow freely.
But if there is no readiness,
any trace of receptivity soon disappears.
That's why I tell stories:
to create readiness,
to nudge the people toward a welcome awakening."
-Matthew 13:10-13 MSG

Don't assume you already know your role
in a story that is still being told.

All Jesus did that day was tell stories—
a long storytelling afternoon.
His storytelling fulfilled the prophecy:
I will open my mouth and tell stories;
I will bring out into the open things hidden
since the world's first day.
—Matthew 13:34-35 MSG

There are a lot of strong
first chapters that start well.

That's good.

But staying in the story
and finishing it well is what counts.

Untold stories that have yet to be spoken.

Unheard songs longing to be sung.

Unseen art eager to fill the empty canvas.

Each waits on us, unwilling to be born until
we're capable of ushering them into existence.

What will come to life on your canvas today?

Rather than ask your art to teach a lesson,
let it be free to tell a story.

Story—not facts—is always a shortcut to the heart.

Our life isn't simply like a story.
It is a story.

Knowing that clarifies the chapter we're in.

Seeing God in it gives our story meaning.

You really can't tell a better story than you're living.

The trajectory of your life affects
the trajectory of your art.

The heart of a story always begins
with the heart of the storyteller.

When you know God has even bigger plans
than you for what's ahead,
there's no longer the need
to try and control your story.

God loves great stories.

His favorites, however,
aren't the ones we write,
paint, or sing.

They are the stories we're living.

May we live the kind of lives
that future generations will tell
as bedtime stories to inspire their children.

Some stories offer a way to unplug from reality.

The better stories usher us into a deeper reality.

Before your stories can take readers
to fantastical places,
you must go there first.

We underestimate stories
when we see them as just
an escape from reality
or a way to teach a lesson.

The best ones help us see our stories
—the ones we're living—
in new ways.

Stuck

Feeling stuck?

If you want a better story,
change the chapter you're in.

You won't get different results
until you try something different.

Your art can't take people to new places
if you're stuck in the same place.

Those who say there's "no way"
presume they can see every possible option.

Their limited vision and lack of faith
stop them from seeing what could be.

God laughs at those limitations,
giving us eyes to see the unseen and countless ways
for impossible dreams to become reality.

When stuck in our art, it's rarely
due to a lack of creativity.

It's usually a prompt to live more
before trying to create more.

An invitation to engage with others
before jumping in to create for others.

In creativity, the status quo
quickly becomes stagnant.

Three reasons we can get stuck on a project:

1) We need to live more
before trying to create more.

2) We don't feel 100 percent qualified or ready.
No one ever is.

3) We approach our creativity alone
when God invites us to enter into it
together with him.

Do you feel stuck in your creativity?

What's not working in our art
is often a warning signal of what's
not working in our lives.

Start there.

Don't let familiarity with your talents
lead to formula in your creations.

It's easy to feel stuck in your story when dreams
haven't come true, risks haven't paid off,
and all outcomes are uncertain.

But this chapter doesn't get to
define you or your future.

Only God does.

When you find something that works,
don't pour concrete over the process.

Forcing future art into past patterns is formula.

And formula never moves you forward.

There's no flexibility to see in new ways.

It leads to stuck artists and stale art.

At times we all feel stuck in our story.

The middle of the "not yet" is that place where dreams haven't come true, risks haven't paid off, and the outcome is far from certain.

It's also the place where God does some of his best creativity.

All artists have moments
of staring at a blank canvas.

That comes with the territory when you're
blazing new trails and exploring new ideas.

But there's another, deeper cause.

When your art is stuck, it can be a sign that
the story you're living in has grown stagnant.

If so, pause on the project.

Go live more. Awaken your heart.
Then create more.

Success

Creating with God is success.

When we enter into our art with God,
success happens as we create—
not later based on external events.

Let this sink in.

The art you create with God
is successful before anyone sees it.
Even if no one sees it.

Believing this allows you to create
from a place of success
rather than in pursuit of success.

Trust GOD from the bottom of your heart;
don't try to figure out everything on your own.
Listen for GOD's voice in everything you do,
everywhere you go;
he's the one who will keep you on track.
—Proverbs 3:5-6 MSG

Want success?

Start by focusing on
how you create rather than
how it performs in the market.

What skill or activity makes you come alive?

God gave you that interest for
the two of you to pursue together.

Rather than expect your passion
to result in acclaim, validation, or income,
what if you defined success as
doing what you love with God...
and that was enough?

Success isn't determined by
others' responses or even
your own expectations.

It simply comes down to this:
Did you pursue what you love with God?

If so, rest in that success.

There is no secret elixir for success.

Constantly seeking it will
only leave you exhausted.

And there's no correlation between
good art and burnt-out artists.

The world's definition of success is
always changing and slightly out of reach.

The only thing it creates is
stress and striving.

Get off that treadmill.

The reality is, if you're pursuing
your dreams and creativity with God,
you're already succeeding wildly
in what matters most.

Do that and stay expectant for what follows.

Rather than chase success,
chase big ideas with God.

Success isn't inherently good...or bad.

When it happens, enjoy it.
And don't be changed by it.

Know that an external blip of victory or validation
isn't enough to sustain your art
or your heart over time.

Nor is it ever the main reason
to do what you're doing.

Whether the world applauds
or not, keep creating.

It matters.

In spite of what some promise,
no formula guarantees quick success.

Mastering an art form
requires time and sacrifice.

Along the way, it will become clear
your gifting is less about you
and more for others.

And true success?

It isn't about popularity
but simply pursuing your passion with God.

Time

You can't be running behind
when you're running with God.

Don't believe the lie that time is scarce.

The Creator of time will give you enough time
for what he's stirred you to pursue.

It's amazing how God is always on time,

yet never in a hurry.

How do you make your art both timely and timeless
when it seems there's not even time
to complete your projects?

Overcome the illusion of scarcity
—and give your art an eternal spark—
by inviting the Creator of time
into your creative process.

What is done in union with God
has the power to transcend you
and ripple far beyond this moment in time.

What you measure reflects what you value.

What you value reveals where you spend your time.

Where you spend time sets the trajectory of your life.

When we feel behind in our dreams
it's because we measure time
based on our clock rather than God's.

There is never an expiration date
on the promises and dreams God gives us.

He will see them through.

Yet they rarely play out as we expect.

The journey becomes more enjoyable
when we trade rigid expectations
for an expectancy of what God is up to.

Transformation

External shifts are easier to see
but are first fueled by unseen internal transformation.

Here's a phrase we can all do without:
"I'm not perfect, you know."

Yes, we do know.

Rather than excuse our broken places,
let's ask God to heal our fractures.

The goal isn't perfection.

It's to be free from what holds us back.

We seek efficiency and ease.

God seeks our transformation.

When we interpret life through that lens,
our days don't become easier,
but they do start to make more sense.

The busier our lives get, the more we begin
to measure who we are by what we do.

But that's a trap.

Those metrics fail to measure what matters most.

God desires our internal transformation
over any external performance.

Being always precedes doing.

Our art won't transcend us
until we allow God to transform us.

The art always follows the heart of the artist.

God's offer is always relational.

How to be more rather than do more.

Trueness

As you pursue your art,
take your cues from the Creator.

His words gave birth to light, stars,
mountains, oceans, and life.

He created out of trueness—
without regard to how we'd later label what was made.

Approach your art with the same freedom.

Let it simply reflect what is true.

Discovered truth is greater than delivered truth.

God didn't create Christian mountains,
Christian oceans, or Christian elephants.

He made each of these original creations in trueness.

Do the same when you create.

Categorizing and creating aren't the same thing.

The world loves to label and limit things.

Never start the creative process
with those artificial constraints.

Create from a place of trueness.

No limits.

Then let others, if they want,
try to label what's never been done before.

Unknown

How would your life change
if you practiced gratitude
in the midst of the unknown
rather than making gratitude
dependent on an outcome?

Instead of
"I'm grateful when things go my way,"
shift to "I'm grateful now, before all is well,
because God is always a good Father."

Unless you choose to forever
stay in a small story,
you have to undertake adventures
where you're no longer the expert.

If you want to create something new,
go somewhere new.

The most engaging art is created by those
willing to spend time and be comfortable
in the unknown, in-between, and not yet.

We long to be fully known,
yet feel completely unknown.

We try to fill that emptiness with control
to avoid more unknown.

But we can't control the next minute.

So we feel unknown and out of control.

Yet even in the unknown,
we are fully known by God.

As long as you keep both feet
firmly planted in the known,
you remain in the story that has been.

Your first step into the unknown
is the start of a new story,
the first page of the not yet.

Just be sure you take that step
at God's prompting and
with him lighting your path.

It's amazing how tensions and worry
over the unknown
fade when you focus on God
rather than the problem.

When you don't demand answers or outcomes,
you gain the ability to take things in
without being taken out by them.

Once you know God is
inviting you into more,
you have a choice.

You can run with him or run from him.

Upgrade

The best way to take your creativity to a new level
is by following God into new frontiers.

The change in you will change your art.

We tend to want the thing we lack.

If only we had that upgrade,
we believe all would be well.

That "one thing" may be more money,
more time, greater success, or better health.
If only we were younger . . . or older.
The list goes on.

Yet the people who have
that very thing we feel would change
everything know it isn't the game changer.

They're wishing for the one thing someone else has.

We're all becoming.
But we are enough and have enough to begin now.

Validation

You'll be amazed how high your creations will fly
when they no longer have to carry you.

Your art doesn't make you.

You make your art.

Your art doesn't validate you.

Only God has the power to do that.

Your creations are only as free as you are.

When you first discovered what you love doing,
there was no striving, no fear,
and no need for outside validation.

There's never a good reason
to add these ingredients later.

Rejection of your art may mean
that person or group just doesn't get it.
Or perhaps wasn't who God chose to carry it forward.

On the other hand, maybe your vision
or craft needs a lot more work.

The right posture is one of both
hope (for what's to come) and
humility (for what you can learn).

When you give anyone or anything other than God
the power to validate your creativity,
you set yourself up for striving and disappointment.

Your creativity isn't your proving ground.

It's your "passion ground."

Let your art invite others into your passions...
not bear the burden of validating you.

When you discover your truest identity,
people and projects lose their power
to validate, limit, or define you.

Creating something new is a hard,
risky, vulnerable endeavor.

But rather than wait for others to validate
(or invalidate) your art, aim higher.

Ask God what he thinks of your gifting.
Listen to his kind but honest response.

There is no truer or more
meaningful validation than that.

Over time, we end up chasing after approval
rather than our original dreams.

We may have forgotten our dreams, but God hasn't.

Perhaps it's time to start chasing those dreams again...
with the One who first gave them to us.

Elevate your art by remembering
why God invited you to create.

Drag it down by expecting
it to validate you.

Don't let the world's response to your art
validate or invalidate you as an artist.

Outside metrics never accurately measure internal gifting.

In a culture where everyone is a critic,
it's easy to lose heart.

But where the world diminishes, God replenishes.

When others say what isn't possible,
rest in God's endless possibilities.

Vine

I am the true vine, and my Father is the gardener.
He cuts off every branch in me that bears no fruit,
while every branch that does bear fruit he prunes
so that it will be even more fruitful.
You are already clean because of the word I have spoken to you.
Remain in me, as I also remain in you.
No branch can bear fruit by itself; it must remain in the vine.
Neither can you bear fruit unless you remain in me.
I am the vine; you are the branches.
If you remain in me and I in you, you will bear much fruit;
apart from me you can do nothing.
If you do not remain in me,
you are like a branch that is thrown away and withers;
such branches are picked up, thrown into the fire and burned.
If you remain in me and my words remain in you,
ask whatever you wish, and it will be done for you.
—John 15:4-7 NIV

If we remain connected to the vine,
we will accomplish great things and bear much fruit.

But if we do not, we can do nothing.

Not do pretty well.

Not pull it together in our own strength.

Nothing.

Abiding isn't simply surviving.

It is staying connected to God's vibrant abundance.

Doing things for God is the opposite of
entering into what God does for you.
—Galatians 3:12 MSG

Vision

It's impossible to create something you can't first see.

Open the eyes of their hearts,
and let the light of Your truth flood in.
Shine Your light on the hope
You are calling them to embrace.
Reveal to them the glorious riches
You are preparing as their inheritance.
—Ephesians 1:18 VOICE

Winging it might be required on occasion,
but it isn't the best long-term strategy
for soaring to new heights.

Ask God for eyes to see the unseen.

To see colors that have never been until this moment.

To see the power of his light overcoming the darkness.

To see the hearts of those you are creating for.

And to see God's intimate involvement
in your creativity.

Our creations can't help but possess our DNA.

It's unavoidable.

What's created in our own strength
possesses our weakness.

In a mythic sense, where we haven't gone,
our creations will stumble.

The vision of your projects and art
will be clouded by your blind spots.

An unexamined life leads to shallow creativity.

The more you know your heart,
the deeper your art can take others.

Wisdom

Wisdom begins with respect for the Lord,
and understanding begins with knowing the Holy One.
— Proverbs 9:10 NCV

A big microphone doesn't signify
the speaker has big ideas.

Loud doesn't make something worth listening to.

A person's title doesn't mean their words are true.

Train your ears to hear what matters
and tune out the numbing noise of nothingness.

God often draws us into places
that lead to the end of our understanding . . .
because that's the beginning of wisdom.

When the Creator of
stars, stallions, and sunsets
offers to reveal
marvelous, great, unsearchable,
and remarkable things (Jeremiah 33:3),
his generosity should set our hearts racing.

When we start with God, he gives us wisdom.

But he also gives us something far more valuable:
himself.

With

And I heard a loud voice
from the throne saying,
"Look! God's dwelling place is now among
the people, and he will dwell with them.
They will be his people, and God himself
will be with them and be their God."
—Revelation 21:3 NIV

We are not called
to do things for God
unless we're first willing
to do those things with God.

Pursuing your art with God is
beautifully disruptive and immensely freeing.

It's the exact opposite of
getting things done in your own strength
or following a formula for success.

God calls his sons and daughters
to graduate from the baby pool
and be wave riders in uncharted waters
that can only be navigated with him.

Stay with God.
Take heart;
Don't quit.
I'll say it again:
Stay with God!
—Psalm 27:14 MSG

We can know a lot about God
and still miss pursuing
our life and dreams with him.

There is so much God wants
to reveal to us and initiate in us.

But the pages of those stories will
remain blank until we pursue them with God.

Our gifting isn't primarily so
we can do things for God—
that's performance-based living.

Our gifting is an invitation to do
what we love with God—
that's relational-based living.

When we embrace life with God,
we never again do life on our own.

We trade isolation for fellowship.

That is the story of with.

God doesn't need your help
as much as he wants your heart.

Whenever you start to focus more on
your talents and gifts than on him,
you miss the main invitation.

Which is to pursue them together.
With him.

For our art to transform others,
it must first transcend us.

That's why God's invitation is
to create with him
rather than in isolation.

Wonder

A mirror reflects what is.

Art can do more.
It reveals what could be.

Before you create, be curious.

Wonder comes before work.

"What if?" is the best first question.

Children sing loud, color outside the lines,
and imagine the impossible.

But as they grow, their unbounded creativity shrinks.

As artists, we must recapture our early awe.

Pablo Picasso said, "It takes a long time to grow young."

Begin becoming young today.

With God, the priority is always
presence over performance,
intimacy over independence,
and wonder over worry.

Choose wonder.

If you're not sure how, try this:
Be expectant for how God will come through.
Lose expectations for how it will happen.
Embrace love over fear.
Create something beautiful

That's a really good start.

Writers

The world doesn't need more stories
from exhausted, striving storytellers.

Focusing on outside metrics
to evaluate the success of your art each day
is a bit like staring at a scoreboard
while missing the actual game.

A hyper focus on the stats
doesn't make a better story.

Writers—your stories matter.

But don't lose focus about which stories God loves most.

The best stories in heaven won't be ones on bookshelves.

They will be the stories of our lives
told around campfires with fellow travelers.

That doesn't mean we shouldn't tell great stories now.

Just that we should be about the business
of living even greater ones.

As writers, our characters are limited by our limitations.

There's a tendency for authors to measure
their productivity by sharing their word count...
how many words they wrote that day.

It's a bit like someone describing a vacation
by saying they took 3,000 steps a day.

Yes, it's specific, measurable data.
And it says nothing about the actual trip.

You can't measure a vacation, a dream,
or a story with a number.

Volume doesn't reflect quality.

A better goal for writers is this:
Make each word earn its place on the page.

Count less and create more.

Yes

Is it hard to say no when people ask
for your creative insights and time...
even when your life is at full capacity?

If so, give yourself permission to
politely say no anyway.

The continual yes to one more thing
comes at too high a price when the cost
is lost family time and soul care.

Don't give your yes to a large project
before fully counting the cost.

When it comes to time and cost,
double what you think it will take.

Even then, you're likely underestimating it.

That doesn't mean you should pass on it.
But do see it clearly before committing.

You

What God has given you is beyond you,
for you, and never up to you.

Don't define yourself by personality tests.

They measure the status quo but have no ability
to predict the new creation God is inviting you to be.

The real test is not who you were yesterday
—or even right this second—
but who you are becoming.

Many look to their art for success.

It's actually a mirror.

If you like what's being reflected back at you through your art, pursue it further.

If not, pursue yourself further.

Either way, the state of your art always reflects the state of your heart.

What is it that you and you alone were born to do?

Do that . . . together with God.

What you create reflects
key aspects of who you are.

Over time, these various pieces come together
to reveal a larger mosaic—
built from every song, book, painting,
and decision you make.

It's worth knowing the larger story your art is telling
. . . and pursuing it with intention.

So often creativity is a game of You vs. Yourself.

Will it be the You of self-reliance or the
You who longs to co-create with God?

The answer plays out in infinite ways each day—
but it is a choice.

You're either doing what you love to do
on your own or with God.

No one is ordinary.

God infused you with a unique way of seeing life.
He gave you specific gifting.

Approach your creativity from that perspective.

The goal isn't to create more like others.

It is to let your art blaze with originality.

Losing your unique voice to achieve success,
especially by chasing the latest trend, isn't wise.

All that tends to create is pressure and repetition.
More conformity than creativity.

Instead, produce original art—
the kind that can only come from you.

Do it even if no one is asking for it . . . yet.
Do it by simply being you.

Self-doubt. Self-help.
Self-made. Self-centered.

Imagine how high your art could soar
if it wasn't quite so focused on . . . you.

A shift happens when God
is invited into the creative process.

By entering into it together,
your art is given an eternal spark
that transcends "self."

This Book is Far Better Because of
the Insights, Encouragement, Prayers,
and Gifting of the Following:

Kellye Arnold

Greyson Arnold

Hope Arnold

Chase Arnold

Kristy Cambron

Karen Christakis

Lorie DeWorken

Flourish (Mindy & Jenny)

Erin Healy

Amy Hudgens

Kristen Ingebretson

Gale Jones

There Is More

Pursuing life and creativity with God is beautifully disruptive and immensely freeing. It begins with knowing God as both Creator and Father...and ourselves as his sons and daughters.

If you're tired of trying to get things done in your own strength or make success happen by following yet another formula, that's good. Because there is a better way. One that will awaken your heart...and your art.

As a fellow traveler,
I hope you'll join me in that journey.

To discover more, visit **withallen.com**

For free daily readings on God and Creativity, go to:
withallen.com/sign-up